Editorial Reviews

"Forest has written a powerful and transcendent account of addiction, trauma, and how they can be overcome. His quest for a life filled with joy is one that speaks to everyone...this is one of the most profoundly fresh, honest and - yes - hopeful books I have ever read. It will change your life."
--Sebastian Junger, Author of *The Perfect Storm, War* and *Tribe*

"This book is a beautifully crafted adventure story into the power of opening ourselves to bliss, ecstasy and ... 'fierce grace.'"
-- **John Perkins,** Author of *The World is As You Dream It* and *Confessions of an Economic Hitman*

"Ananda Forest has always been a great explorer of life. He has gone from the depths of suffering and addiction to navigating his way along a path that brought him to the power of a variety of spiritual traditions which teach all healing comes from love. This book is brilliantly written straight from Ananda's soul and heart to make a connection with you to inspire you to heal your old traumas. 'Here for The Joy' helps us flow from suffering to a life and joy and provides the tools that helped Ananda walk through the darkness to a life of joy."
--Sandra Ingerman, MA, shamanic teacher and author of 13 books, including **Walking in Light and the Book of Ceremony.**

"Here for the Joy is a spiritual growth memoir that models how every human being can achieve freedom and deep, abiding joy.
--Kristine Morris, *Clarion Reviews*

HERE
FOR THE
JOY

HERE
FOR THE
JOY

A Memoir of Survival,
Addiction Recovery, Spiritual
Enlightenment, and In-Depth
Personal Transformation

Ananda Forest

I offer this book up at the lotus feet

of

Mata Amritanandamayi and Neem Karoli Baba,

Amma and Baba,

Mom and Dad

The soul is here for its own joy.
—Rumi

ACKNOWLEGEMENTS

Where does the thread of gratitude begin? Andrew Harvey, who was, I suspect, impatient with my endless storytelling, told me finally, "You should write a book." A few years later, a little more encouragingly, my friend, Judy Greenberg, said the same thing. Finally, a YouTube ad clinched it: "You have my permission to write a book."

Early readers were encouraging. My sister, Anne, blasted through a rough draft in a day. My brother, Joshua said he loved it. Sebastian Junger commented on my "extraordinary vision." I cannot express how crucial these early kind words were, wind beneath my wings. Many other friends read it as well and I am so grateful for your time and attention and wise words.

John Carlson compared it to a 21st century On the Road. My men's group was incredibly generous with their time and support. Troy, Elliot, Raph, Guru Dharm, Shawn, Jason, Eric, Bill and Peter— thank you, thank you, thank you! Your kind words and insights meant so much. You walked with me through the darkness. And one last word: Waheguru!!!

Others had helpful ideas as well. Cara Benedetto told me where to end the book. Nancy Crompton guided me on how to begin, starting with title layout. Sebastian told me I was writing two books and told me I needed an editor, perhaps the best advice of all.

I must thank Lily Golden from the bottom of my heart. Although some pages of the manuscript were almost unreadable due to the blizzard of pencil lead, she helped me turn *Here for the Joy* into a real book. Thank you! The folks at *Archangel Ink,* Rob and Kristie took me the next step in self-publishing with their kind, wise and expert guidance. You guys are amazing!

And then there is Gog. My man! Thanks to your inspiration, I am standing here with my book in my hands!

If I have left anyone out, please accept my apologies. The proof is in the pudding: I could not, would not have been able to write this book by myself.

Finally, I must thank my wife, partner, best friend and cosmic playmate, iishana Artra. Without her, there would be no book. Her extraordinary patience, wisdom and compassion over the ten years we have been together in this life created the chrysalis from which the butterfly could emerge. She intuitively recognized the book was coming before I did and always gave me space and support, by turn, during the birthing process. Her editing suggestions were always right on as was her guidance about publishing, promotion and the countless other details that go into creating a book. Thank you, my love.

Table of Contents

Preface

We live in a dark time. Although we may find hope and enthusiasm in the smaller spheres of our personal lives, it is hard to find a lot of optimism about the world. Pick up a newspaper, check your phone. Things do not look good. The long-term prognosis for the economy, the climate, the planet, is one of pessimism and gloom. Yeats' prophecy from a hundred years ago, "The best lack all conviction while the worst are full of passionate intensity," seems only more true now.

In times such as these, concepts like joy or bliss can seem naïve. Yet, eight hundred years ago, in a time easily as terrible as ours, Rumi insisted that "The soul is here for its own joy." The fundamental purpose of a human being, he insisted, is to find and create joy. And he lived to see his country invaded by Mongols, his beloved teacher murdered.

The Hindu tradition, which grapples fearlessly with human suffering, holds that the fundamental truth of God and the human soul is *satchitananda*: truth, consciousness, bliss. A sequence is implied: first we experience the unabridged truth of existence, the bottom line of all bottom lines. Only then do we become fully conscious, awake, aware of

1

how it really is.   And then, what is our response, our state of mind? *Ananda*, pure joy.

Even Jesus, no stranger to a really bad day, insisted to the end, "Except ye become as little children, ye shall not enter into the kingdom of heaven." And probably the ultimate criticism of joy is that it is childish. When so many things are going so wrong, only a child would consider his own joy to be the most important thing. We are often led to believe that giving up such joy is one of the things about the "Real world" we have to accept.

The most forceful Twentieth-century advocate for the primacy of joy is probably Joseph Campbell.   His most famous phrase, "Follow your bliss," is so familiar it has become a cliché, often followed by an eye roll or a knowing smirk. Not so different from "When pigs have wings."

To follow one's bliss is viewed in the main as frivolous, foolish, even dangerous. The word "bliss," meaning "perfect happiness" or "great joy," is in itself viewed as childish or improbable. It is rarely used by teachers or professors, even less by career counselors or employers. Like sex, it is something better not spoken of in public, a matter of private, personal inquiry. Just don't expect too much.

What Campbell actually said, is a bit fuller than the meme version:
 [F]ollow your bliss and don't be afraid, and doors will open where you didn't know they were going to be. If you follow your bliss, doors will open for you that wouldn't have opened for anyone else.

This original quote is from Bill Moyers' interview of Joseph Campbell for the PBS series, *Joseph Campbell and the Power of Myth*, in 1988.   It is the core of a larger anthem of hope and liberation which, when I first heard it just after graduating from Yale Law School, hit me harder than anything I had learned in the previous three years.

However, just as the wisdom of the *Tao Te Ching*, another paradigm-shifting text for me, was boiled down to "Go with the flow" and worn

2

into banality by generations of Californians, Joseph Campbell's hard won wisdom has been processed and largely cast aside. Few recall that this quote was the result of a lifetime of great passion and hard work. From boyhood, Joseph Campbell loved folk tales and myths. Instead of giving up "childish things," he persisted in following this passion into adulthood and eventually received tenure at Sarah Lawrence College, where he wrote *The Hero with a Thousand Faces* and introduced the world to the idea of a universal "hero's journey." By following his joy, he found doors opened where there had been no doors before.

Campbell's clarion call, his vision of a pathway to freedom, has been largely forgotten in the generation since his passing. We don't seem to have much time for joy these days.

But when I first heard those words spoken by him in 1988, they called to something deep within me, a call I have been unable to avoid answering ever since, in spite of all the good advice I've received from a life of privileged education and opportunity. In over twenty years spent at America's "best" schools, not one teacher or advisor ever encouraged me to follow my bliss. Instead I was directed to follow my talents, do what I was good at, go where the jobs were.

To focus on joy for its own sake in the midst of accelerating global crisis feels a little in bad taste. Or completely missing the point. The general attitude seems to be "We live in desperate times and should act accordingly." There is little time now for joy, certainly not as one's main purpose.

But what if one were to engage in a fantastic experiment? What if one were to take Joseph Campbells's advice at face value and use it as the guidelines for one's life? What if one were to double down on this command as bedrock wisdom that has persisted around the world for millennia? This is what I have done for the past twenty-five years.

Follow your bliss and you will come to the end of the Way. Bliss -- or joy, as I prefer to call it-- is the heart struck by the truth of its own

3

nature. The Sri Yantra, the ancient Hindu symbol for OM, the vibration of the Universe, represents this note sustained at its fullest possible amplitude. You don't need to believe or understand this. All you need to do is to follow the smile of your own joy. As Mary Oliver so kindly observes, "You only have to let the soft animal of your body love what it loves." You only need to move toward your own joy as a plant's leaves seek the light, as her roots seek moisture. Only in this way will you, can you, discover what is written on your own seed packet, who you really are.

What I discovered is that joy is not merely a childish thing, fragile and fleeting. Joy is a lion. Joy can move mountains, create galaxies. Anything worth doing will soar higher, fly further, dig deeper, if it is fueled by joy. If you are serious about saving the world (or yourself), joy will be required. And the really good news about joy? It's what we are made of. But I am getting ahead of myself.

Chapter 1

The Seed is Planted

When I was born, I was named George, after my father and his father and his father and his father, but it was my grandmother who caught me. Not when I first came out of my mom. I was pulled out of her with a set of tongs by an obstetrician. No, three days later, when I still hadn't had a bowel movement. Everyone was getting a little worried. No poop! But then, my grandmother recalled with a large smile, I "exploded" in her arms. She was a safe place to land.

And she continued to be a safe place for the rest of her life. When my mother was overwhelmed with episodes of PTSD from her own violent upbringing, she and my father both became afraid for me. We were living in Cambridge at the time. My dad had just finished med school at Harvard and was deep in his psychiatric internship. My mom, struggling with postpartum depression, was alone with me for hours every day, day after day. The breaking point came when I was seven months old and she hurled a telephone at me.

They flew me out to Michigan after that and left me with my father's mother for a few weeks. Maybe that would help. It did, but not in the way my parents intended. My mother's violence towards me continued, but my grandmother always said that's when I became her "fourth child," after her eldest, Joanna, my dad, and their younger brother, Henry. I was her favorite.

My first memory of her begins on a plane. I was three and flying out to Michigan so my mom could get another break. I had a window seat and my nose was pressed against the glass. The flash of sunlight off the wings, the roaring blur of the propellers, enthralled me. I was even more amazed by what came next. The forward rush of the plane, its acceleration pressing me against the seat like a huge hug, the sudden weightlessness as we rose off the ground.

And that's what my grandmother was like—an embracing rush of joy and generosity. She was always so happy to see me! She made me feel like the center of the universe, the best thing that could happen to a person. She asked me what my favorite foods were and made them for me. Hamburgers and grilled cheese sandwiches. I learned from her that food tasted best out of a cast iron skillet. I remember from that early trip, looking up at the black iron handle, extending out over my head, and knowing something good was in there.

I always called her "Grandmother." In many families, grandmothers are named by the first grandchild's attempts to say her name. My mother's mother was always called Baba, after my elder cousin's garbled "Barbara." But I was a precise child, always trying to do the right thing. When my father's mother, Sue, told me she was my grandmother, that's what I called her. Grandmother. And that's how she was referred to for the rest of her life.

Those early childhood visits became the model for our relationship. Once or twice a year, for the next forty-six years, I would stay with her for a week or two, even after I left home for college. And our visits expanded as I did—from providing food and shelter and a warm embrace when I was small, to exploring my shifting interests as I grew. When I was twelve, in 1971, and wanted to change the world, she talked politics with me and took me to meet my senator in Washington D.C.. Later, as I became more mystical, we visited art museums and she gave me my first copy of the Tao Te Ching.

It made sense that my soul would receive its mandate while I was with her. I was twenty-nine, fresh out of law school, but I was just as scared and lost as I had been on my first trip to visit my grandmother. I hated the law, but was unsure which way to turn. Going to stay with Sue was always a refuge.

We were watching *Joseph Campbell and the The Power of Myth* in the summer of 1988 when this PBS-broadcast swan song brought Campbell to the attention of millions of Americans. My grandmother had long known of Joe (as Bill Moyers, the PBS interviewer, refers to Professor Campbell). When Campbell's best known book, *The Hero with a Thousand Faces*, was first published in the late forties, my grandmother had her deep Episcopalian faith shaken by Campbell's insistence that the story of Jesus was no different than a thousand pagan myths that preceded him. Look beneath cultural specifics, Campbell argued, and you will find that one hero's journey is very like another's: all expressions of the human soul's natural evolution.

This view did not sit well with what Sue had learned in over four decades of going to church. She recalls falling into a disturbed sleep after finishing the book and dreaming of being alone in an enormous pitch-black room. Out of the silence came a deep and soothing voice, "My child, don't you see? All my myths are true."

My grandmother was telling me this story in her Franconia, New Hampshire summer home as *The Power of Myth* began. Bill Moyers is talking about the hero's journey with Joseph Campbell and Sue is nodding in agreement. This is not new to her. As the two men unpack this idea of a universal human adventure, Campbell leans back in his chair and attempts to sum up a lifetime's work:

7

Follow your bliss. If you do follow your bliss, you put yourself on a kind of track that has been there all the while waiting for you, and the life you ought to be living is the one you are living. When you can see that, you begin to meet people who are in the field of your bliss, and they open the doors to you. I say, follow your bliss and don't be afraid, and doors will open where you didn't know they were going to be. If you follow your bliss, doors will open for you that wouldn't have opened for anyone else.

There was no pause button, no way to rewind these words. My grandmother and I both sat up and looked into each other's eyes. Had Campbell just said what we thought he had said? His wisdom was so simple, so obvious, so intuitively true. And yet it was so far from what anyone had ever said to either of us. I have no memory of the rest of that episode or even the series. My soul had just received its marching orders.

It would take another six years for me to begin to consciously follow those orders, but from that moment until my grandmother's death seven years later, she and I would often refer back to that evening. It was a watershed for both of us, but in different ways. For me, these words pointed the way forward, told how my life would unfold. For my grandmother, they were an affirmation of long ago choices—marrying an archaeologist instead of the banker her father would have chosen, accompanying her husband on digs in the mountains of Mexico instead of hosting dinner parties. That feeling Campbell spoke of had led her away from her deep Republican roots and toward Adlai Stevenson and his more hopeful view of human nature and, later, to Dr. King. She was in the crowd that summer day in 1963 when those words rang out— "I have a dream…". Sue had always believed in the Dream and Campbell's words came as a final affirmation.

Although I was inspired by Campbell's wisdom, I was also held by the gravitational pull of my own life. As a recent graduate from Yale Law School and as the namesake of several generations of Harvard-trained over-achievers who viewed inclusion in *Who's Who* as a natural right, I had some more immediate fish to fry. Although I had intuitively

8

followed Joe's advice by turning my back on a lucrative and high-profile career in law to teach at a private school in Brooklyn, I was inwardly torn by doubt and shame. I had followed my bliss by deciding that sharing my love for fiction with kids would be a lot more fun than writing legal memos. However, a voice in my head kept telling me I was a loser, a failure, retreating to a world of children rather than toughing it out in law or politics. And besides, what secondary school teacher ever wound up in *Who's Who*?

I hit the wall with teaching after six years. Even though the private school I taught at was known as progressive—there were no grades, students called faculty by their first names, teachers could select pretty much any book they wanted to teach—I began to see that, under this liberal frosting, I was teaching children to endure boredom under florescent lights, come and go according to bells, work hard in hopes of getting into a good college (that would bring more of the same). Looking into the windows of the office building across the street from my eighth story classroom, I could see "vice presidents" at Morgan Stanley doing the same thing: sitting in front of word processors, bored out of their minds, counting the minutes until they could go home.

Chapter 2

Following my Bliss

In the summer of '94, I left Brooklyn and moved upstate with my wife, Nancy, and one-year-old son, Kirby. Nancy and I met in English class at Oberlin, American Romanticism, thirteen years earlier. She looked like a Modigliani, but my favorite view was from the back, the way her dark hair curled around her ears, along her pale slender neck. We connected over coffee and Melville. She didn't care for him much, but her laser mind, cutting through nonsense, was exhilarating. She was a militant feminist and that turned me on, too, the challenge, the edge. We both loved diners and nineteenth century New England and would lose ourselves in endless riffs about Hawthorn and our shared backgrounds, our Puritan roots. Looking into her eyes for the first time was bliss.

After a year-long courtship, we finally made love in a field in upstate New York. Looking up into the blue sky after, golden rod swaying around us, the buzz of crickets, I knew I was home. This is where we first connected physically in 1982 and it's where we moved twelve years later after we both grew weary of urban life. After Kirby's birth, we wanted to own our home, but the only housing we could afford on teachers' pay was a tiny rundown apartment a block from the projects.

Nightly gunfire, crack vials on the doorstep. Maybe life in the country could provide what the city could not.

The "ah-ha" moment in our decision to move was when we found our house, a nine hundred square foot "fixer-upper," on a remote dirt road south of Cambridge, New York. We bought it outright for $40,000, what would have been the down payment for a co-op or condo in our old neighborhood. Here we were set in a Grandma Moses landscape. We even had a stream across the road, winding among cows and apple trees. When I first heard it, though, the steady rushing of water reminded me of endless traffic on the Brooklyn-Queens Expressway.

The place needed a lot of work, but Nancy's dad, who had built their nearby house, knew all about that. He helped me hone my carpentry skills and gave me my first lessons in wiring, and hanging sheetrock. Nancy and I had been on many adventures—teaching together, trips to England and Greece, long summers at my family's place in northwest Connecticut—this felt like the next one. We spent hours designing a kitchen, picking out paint colors, just like newlyweds. We settled on an open floor plan— kitchen flowing into dining room flowing into living room. Lots of windows and no interior doors, not even on the bathroom. Nancy grew up that way (more efficient air flow) and I went along. The three of us slept on a king-sized mattress upstairs in a loft space with an enormous skylight. We shared coffee up there every morning, Kirby snuggled in the nearest lap.

During the days, Kirby toddled contentedly around the construction site, surrounded by loving relatives. With a picturesquely collapsing barn nearby and a small swimming pond in the meadow above, not to mention two thousand daffodils planted in the gardens, you could say we were in heaven. Or at least it looked like that.

Nancy knew at ten what she would be when she grew up: a teacher and writer, like her dad. Our move to the country meant it was time for her to upgrade to college teaching. She began sending her resume around, working family contacts, and soon had an adjunct position at nearby Bennington College. She had just published her first book of poetry and showed promise. I, on the other hand, had no idea what I wanted to be when I "grew up." I only knew what I didn't want to do, and that included teaching and practicing law.

Three months into my new life in the country, I was drunk and unable to think of anything more meaningful than to try and seduce my wife's best friend. Even buzzed on three margaritas and making my first clumsy attempt at footsie, I could feel in my gut that no good would come of this. Nancy was sitting right across from me. I decided to keep my foot to myself. But I knew I was on thin ice.

Later that same weekend, as I wandered through the Self Help section of a local bookstore, a single title jumped out: *Do What You Love and the Money Will Follow* (by Marsha Sinetar). The sheer improbability of these words caught my attention. Could it be that simple? This rewording of Joseph Campbell's dictum had my attention. I was desperate, ready to take the leap.

At thirty-five, I had sampled a variety of career paths: written a publishable honors thesis—Behind the Mask: Ritual and Rebellion in Rural Ireland-- as an anthropology major, graduated from law school with lucrative job offers, played in bands in NYC bars, and published poetry and fiction in reputable quarterlies. I had worked as a carpenter and a house painter in the year I took off from law school. I had taught English at a prestigious private school for six years. All of it had led to the same place: boredom and despair.

I knew part of the problem lay in the depression I had inherited from both sides. My father's father had succeeded in killing himself; my mother's mother tried to poison herself and her two daughters. She gave it a good enough try that, while she and my mother and aunt survived, she was put in a mental hospital and her children taken from her. I often felt that, while everyone in my family could have a Harvard decal on their rear car window to boast of their accomplished children, it should be accompanied by a McClean Hospital sticker, to honor the Harvard-affiliated psychiatric hospital in Belmont at which many members of my family had also matriculated.

Shortly after moving to the country with Nancy, I read an article in The New Yorker about Elaine Pagels, the Princeton scholar who was making waves with her writing about the Gnostic gospels, and particularly the *Gospel of Thomas*. Unearthed in 1945, but written as early as 60AD, before any other gospel, Thomas's transcriptions of Jesus's words were radically changing people's perception of what He really said, who He really was. The quote that blew my mind was this saying, attributed to Jesus,

If a man brings forth what is within him, what he brings forth will save him. If he fails to bring forth what is within him, what he fails to bring forth will destroy him.

The world stopped for a moment. The inarguable truth of these words, their gravity, held me. I knew they were true. I knew, also, that this wisdom explained my depression, why after half a lifetime I could not get satisfaction— not from teaching, not from marriage, not from fatherhood. I had not yet brought forth what was truly within me. I also understood that my despair could destroy me.

Encountering Marsha Sinitar's book, soon after reading The New Yorker piece, was a double tap. "Do what you love and the money will follow." These words, of course, echoed Joseph Campbell's instructions about following your bliss. And whatever you called it—bliss, joy, what you love, what is inside you—it doesn't matter. Getting down to it, bringing it forth, whatever it is, is the *only* thing that matters.

I finally had my direction, my true north: Do what I loved. Of course, this direction had been in me all along, but not always clearly seen or trusted. I had long been aware of an inner guidance system: a distinct, warm glowing sensation right behind the navel that occurred whenever I was presented with something I really wanted to do. The reason I did so well in college was because I had only taken courses I knew I would love, not paying attention to requirements or what would look good to grad schools.

However, I didn't always trust this feeling. Other voices could drown it out. Law school was a case in point. There was nothing I loved about that except the acceptance letter. Three of them actually, Harvard, Yale, Columbia. Each one promised safety and success, the Ivy League guarantee, a path free of shame. It's just that the skills law school required used only half my brain, the one that aced standardized tests. My intuition, my dreams, my feelings had no place there.

It was this glow that led me into teaching. I saw how happy Nancy was at St. Ann's School and decided to join her. She didn't care if I was famous and this acceptance provided a refuge just as my grandmother had. But the fun faded and the rolling green fields of Cambridge, New York beckoned. Once in the countryside, though, in a peaceful, rural setting upstate, I ran out of clues. The trail had gone cold.

But now I was going to do what I loved and trust that the money would follow, crazy as that might sound. I didn't have a choice. Nothing else worked. I was halfway through my life. And here it is important to emphasize that I was going to have to pay my own way. There was no trust fund or hard-won grant or crowdsourcing website to underwrite this project. I may have quit my day job in the city, but I had to find a new one.

I believe a fundamental reason people resist the words, "Follow your bliss," is the gut feeling that it can't be done. It isn't realistic. Who's going to pay the bills? And here, again, it is best to go back to Joseph Campbell's original words. He in no way intended his guidance to substitute the directions for a responsible human life. In fact, his original advice was quite modest. He invited people to create a space in their lives to cultivate what lit them up. He called this space a "bliss station," and recommended that everyone create some kind of place in their home, in their lives, that was dedicated purely to that bliss.

A person of immense means could dedicate a big budget, a whole house or property or life, to this endeavor. But what Campbell intended for most of us, I believe, was simply a small dedicated space such as we might set aside for a personal altar or to pursue a hobby. And likewise, the commitment of time could also be partial: an hour a day, on weekends. The point was not that we had to abandon everything and fling ourselves after bliss. The important thing was to say out loud what our joy was, that it was important enough to name and to invest some time in.

So, as I began this project, I still had to find a paying job to cover my costs. I knew I wasn't going to have much to live on for a while. Fortunately, Nancy had grown up in a family of proto-hippies; her home had been built by her and her parents for six thousand dollars. When I first met her, she rolled her eyes when I suggested we go to the supermarket. Her family never went shopping. They grew all their own food.

When I shared my plan to "do what I loved" with Nancy, she had no problem with it. She was not tormented by success and prestige as I was. While she did not aspire to her parents' hardscrabble existence, she could tolerate living on a minimal budget for a while. Nancy was amused by my family's stuffiness, their old school Waspiness; it didn't threaten her. As long as I brought in some money, she didn't mind this shift in direction. In fact, it was right out of Thoreau or Melville, our shared roots. And, if it promised to ease my depression, she was all in.

I found work as a carpenter's assistant for eight dollars an hour with a man named Rod. He was a year older than me. With his beard and pony tail, bushy eyebrows and piercing blue eyes, he looked like an extra from Braveheart. After college, he'd left Albany and turned to his dream to live off the land and work with locally sourced hardwoods. He ploughed with horses and had chickens running through his shop. He was to be my teacher in many ways, but I didn't know that yet.

15

Because we had no mortgage, our nut was minimal. I was free to turn to my personal bliss. The first thing that came to mind was learning how to hunt. I came from a long line of non-hunters and grew up with the most effective anti-hunting polemic ever created—Bambi. Furthermore, I had been raised to think of hunters as Budweiser-swilling yahoos, shooting at anything that moved.

Now I was in another world. The county we had moved to was staunchly pro-gun; the local video store even had a Hunting section, featuring an assortment of films ranging from straight up gun porn, where the "money shot" was a deer or bear in its death throes, to thoughtful documentaries on the feeding and breeding habits of white tail deer. Combining a "when in Rome" attitude with a life-long fascination with guns, I decided to take up hunting. I found a .30.30 lever action at Fred's Guns 'n' Mobil, the gun shop/gas station in town, and started working on my aim in the three acre pasture behind my house.

The first thing I learned was that killing a deer is a lot harder than it sounds. The whitetail deer— the one you often see crossing (or lying dead alongside) roads throughout the Northeast— reached its current stage of evolutionary perfection almost four million years ago. Humans, by contrast, have only been around for 200,000 years. We may be bipedal and packing a big brain, but whitetail deer have been avoiding predators, some a lot bigger and scarier than us, for over three million years. And it shows. On average, only one in six hunters will kill a deer in a given season.

I quickly learned that I was a buffoon in the woods—noisy, smelly and stupid. Everyone—birds, squirrels, deer—knew when I was coming and where I was before I did. Elaborate inter-species alert systems run through every patch of forest, where one animal, as soon as it spies or smells a human, makes a warning sound that is soon picked up and repeated in a variety of animal languages.

If I ever saw a deer, it was usually its white tail, waving in a soon-to-be familiar taunt, as it disappeared over a stone wall or into brush. I had a high-powered rifle and was developing good aim, but what use was that if I couldn't find something to shoot at? I soon realized that it would take some serious schooling before I stood a chance of actually killing one of these animals.

Fortunately, Nancy's dad, our son's namesake, knew how to track. He was the quietest man I ever met. Eldest son of a relentlessly domineering father, he found his way in stoic silence, first as a novelist and college teacher, then as a financial advisor to lower income folks seeking to own their own homes. The treeless wilds of northern Canada was the only place he ever felt at home, but the woods around Cambridge, NY were his second choice.

He showed me how to recognize a deer "rub," the spot on saplings a foot or two off the ground where bucks rub off their "velvet," the soft, fuzzy layer covering the blood vessels and nerves which provide nourishment and protection to the hardening antlers beneath. This annual ritual (all male deer grow a new set of antlers each summer and shed them in winter) tells you where the bucks are. It looks like someone has been going over the bark with a cheese grater

He also showed me the "scrape," a patch of bare earth a couple of feet across where the prospective suitor urinates to tempt available does. If she like what she smells, the doe (or does) will also urinate in the same spot and a conversation of sorts ensues, with each deer taking turns expressing its enthusiasm. Of course, turkeys can leave similar bare patches in their search for acorns. The only way to be sure, Kirby told me with a wink, is to get down on your knees and sniff.

The essence of hunting, though, Kirby senior explained, is patience. While some hunters prefer to stalk, moving slowly and silently through the woods in search of prey, the most effective method is to lie in wait, often for hours. Deer's eyes are extraordinarily attuned to movement and their noses to smell. Not to mention their hearing. Staying low and

17

still is your best bet. Remaining motionless in the early morning dark of November is bone chilling. "The coldest I have ever been," Kirby cautioned.

Also on my bliss list was drinking. I loved to drink, whiskey in particular. It made me feel joyous and free, at least for a while. And, more specifically, I wanted to learn how to make it myself. Familiar with those black and white photos in Jack Daniels ads extolling the simple virtues of its place of origin—Lynchburg, Tennessee—I had finally made a pilgrimage three years earlier.

Returning from a whiskey- and beer-soaked trip to Mardi Gras with some buddies, we decided to stop in at the distillery on the way home. What followed was a how-to seminar on making bourbon: Here are the eleven tractor trailers which arrive each day with the corn. Here are the 40,000-gallon stainless-steel vats where the corn and water mash ferments—the yeast eats the sugar in the corn, releasing alcohol as a waste product. When the alcohol content hits around ten percent, the yeast drowns in its own waste. If you want a higher alcohol content, you have to leave biology and turn to chemistry: distillation.

As we all know water boils at 212 degrees Fahrenheit. The good news, if you want something harder than wine or beer to drink, is that alcohol evaporates at 178 degrees. That twenty-four degree window is the sweet spot for the distiller. Heat your mash (fermented grain) to exactly 178 degrees and the steam will be 99 percent alcohol. Obviously, if you do this at home on your stove, all this fine alcohol will literally vanish in a mist. But, if you have a way to contain and capture the steam...

A still is basically a pressure cooker with a repurposed release valve. Attach a copper tube to the lid, heat the contents to precisely 178 degrees, and pure alcohol vapor will be forced through that tube. Run that tube through cool water and the vapor will condense to alcohol pure enough to set fire to. The technology hasn't changed a lot since the first alchemists searched for the elusive elixir of immortality, the water of

18

life, the water that literally would catch fire. It is no coincidence that the most popular hard liquor in Europe is commonly called aquavite (Latin for "water of life") or that the Celtic root of whiskey, uisge beatha (which morphed in the Middle Ages to usquebaugh and, later, to whiskybae) means the same thing.

This, in a nutshell, was what I learned on the tour of the Jack Daniels distillery. And that Lynchburg was in a dry county. At the tour's end, the clearly inebriated guide offered us our choice of coffee or lemonade. "I'm afraid the only Jack we can offer y'all is what we got in some mustard or barbeque sauce in the shop." He didn't seem at all sad. "Shit," I muttered, "I've walked into an AA meeting."

However, I left with something a lot more valuable than a drink. I now knew how to make the drink myself.

Upstate New York seemed like the perfect place to take the next step. Although it wasn't Appalachia, my new neighborhood—steep wooded hollows, trailers surrounded by derelict barns and cars from long ago— would have fit right in in rural Kentucky. I just needed a partner.

The first and only person to show any interest was Dave. A few years older than me, he had fled the suburbs of New Jersey in his early twenties after college and had spent the last fifteen years honing his skills as a carpenter and all around craftsman and musician. He was not an Ivy League outcast like me. His father was a Syrian born-again evangelical minister whose constant urgings about Christ had forced his eldest son out of the house. The only characteristic Dave shared with his dad was his dark good looks. He had been called "Adonis" in high school and, with his black hair and flashing brown eyes, he still turned heads.

He loved the idea of becoming a moonshiner and had the chops I was lacking: metal working skills, a knowledge of practical chemistry, years of working with his hands. We set up shop in the crumbling barn next to my new house and began our quest to learn the mysteries of distilling.

19

Another passion was working on cars. Since my dad was a professor of psychiatry, the only thing I grew up knowing about cars was how to change a tire. Everything that went on under the hood was a complete mystery. As I began to get to know mechanics through the vagaries of my own vehicles, I came to dread every time my car had a problem. It wasn't just that I had no way of knowing if what the mechanic said was true or not. I also was aware of the enormity of the cultural divide between me in my nice, college boy clothes and the man in the blue, grease-stained jumpsuit deciding my fate. I might be a clever fellow in my own world, but to him I was just another ignoramus too stupid and lazy to ever bother learning anything about the machine that made his life possible. Each time my car had a problem was like being given a negative lottery ticket: how much was I going to get hit up for this time?

While I was in law school, my first car, a 1977 Datsun F-10 that my roommate sold me for $800, died, costing me along the way what felt like thousands of dollars. I decided to take matters into my own hands. When my next car, an '82 Ford Escort, filled with a sweet smelling steam that fogged the windows and made it impossible to drive, I did not take it to a mechanic. Instead, I began burrowing under the dashboard with borrowed tools, following the pool of antifreeze on the floor back to its source—something called a "heater core."

Carrying this strange object, resembling a miniature radiator, triumphantly into the auto parts store like a hunting trophy, I inquired what it was and could I get a new one. I was hooked.

Over the next few years, during summer vacations from teaching, I acquired hundreds of tools, tore down entire car engines and rebuilt and installed three, which all started and ran after I was done. This is immensely satisfying: hundreds of pieces of metal taken apart and then coming back together in a smoking roar. Way beyond guiding a good discussion on Robert Frost. In my new life in upstate New York, I felt ready to hang out my shingle and try to market my services as a mechanic. All I needed in my garage was a grease pit.

A narrow pit or trench over which a vehicle can be driven and conveniently worked on from beneath, grease pits have served as a poor man's lift for generations. Now illegal due to the fact a person can be trapped, burned or suffocated in one, they had long held a deep appeal for me. Never mind the hazards; if I had one, I would no longer have to lie on my back when I wanted to go under a car. All I had to do was climb into the pit—five and a half feet deep, three feet wide, and ten feet long—and I could reach the oil pan or differential with ease.

I set to work on the dirt floor of my garage. After a few days, I discovered why land was so affordable in my neighborhood: "Cossayuna loam," my wife's uncle referred to it with a chuckle, hardpacked clay liberally seeded with boulders. Too hard to dig with a shovel, the dense soil required breaking up with a pick ax. This worked for a few blows until I hit a rock which jarred every joint in my body and made my teeth rattle. After a couple of hours of this abuse, I rented a jack hammer. At least now the playing field was even. Removing the roughly 250 wheelbarrow loads of clay and rocks from that hole was the hardest physical work I had ever done.

My earliest source of joy was music. My parents sang to me at bedtime and I treasured those moments of intimacy. Their songs, "Casey Jones" (Dad) and "Down in the Valley" (Mom) still move me whenever I hear them. My first "Aha" moment with music, though, came when I was six.

After my second brother, Henry, was born in 1965, my parents hired an au pair from Liverpool, Sue Lee, and she brought with her the sounds of her generation—the Beatles, Herman's Hermits, the Beach Boys. "Surfin' USA", that repackaging of Chuck Berry's reworking of the classic twelve bar blues, knocked me out. I wanted more.

Later that summer, on Martha's Vineyard, where my mom's family helped found a summer community in the 1880's, Sue Lee took me and my brothers, John and Henry, down to the closest town to show us a real discotheque, the vogue term for dancehall. Even though it was early in the day and no music would be happening until after dark, I got lucky; a young man was working out on a drum kit in the center of the large, empty space.

I stood in the open French doors at the club entrance, my eyes following the lines of maple flooring as they raced toward the seated figure, his back to us. The young man didn't know we were there and he was really going at it, foot pounding on the kick, sticks flying from the snare to the toms and back, head nodding. He was dressed like a real Beach Boy — madras shorts, a LaCoste shirt, his hair in a flat top crew cut—and the din he was creating poured over me in the most wonderful way. My entire body felt held and I was filled with a warm, pulsing glow.

I forgot who I was, where I was. And then the au pair tugged my hand and we were off to the grocery store. We never spoke of that moment. I was too young to attend a live show. Way past my bedtime. It never occurred to me to mention this revelation to my parents. I had no language for what had just happened. However, from then on, I took every opportunity to listen whenever Sue Lee was playing records or the radio.

And, for the next twenty years, that was my relationship with music: a listener. My family didn't have any musicians in it as far as I knew. We were writers, word smiths, intellectuals. Everyone knew my dad was tone deaf and I seemed to be, too. The idea that music could be about rhythm, also, was completely foreign. All the music my parents listened to was primarily focused on melody. When instruments were presented to us at school, violin, cello and piano were the only options. Drums were never mentioned.

It wasn't until I was halfway through law school, completely miserable, hovering near the bottom of my class, that it occurred to me to take up the bass. I loved the blues. Several of my friends played guitar and keyboards. A bass player was always needed. And, best of all, it only had four strings. "Not too many rocket scientists behind the bass," a buddy observed. Perfect.

So during the most important set of exams in my law school career—second year, first semester—I was out shopping for an electric bass. Even though it would be another three years before I heard Joseph Campbell's words, I was following my bliss—the way music made me feel.

I decided to leave law school for a year. I practiced bass very day, took lessons and was soon in my first band. Although I went on to play in a number of bands, gigging in small Manhattan clubs, I was never able to give it enough time. If the route to Carnegie Hall was "Practice, practice, practice," I never got past P-r-a. I was starting too late in life, wasn't good enough, music wasn't a serious profession, I had to earn money... The excuses piled up.

Now, however, with my new mandate—Do what you love...— music had to have a place. A bunch of my new upstate friends were in a drumming circle—mostly djembes and congas—why couldn't I join? I met them through Nancy's parents, who served as mentors to a lot of younger urban refugees near Cambridge. They had all left the city and college degrees behind to pursue lives working with their hands. Among them were Rod, who gave me my first job upstate, and Dave, my moonshining partner. Also among them were Scott and John, former NYC set designers, who had just finished building a round cordwood house near Cambridge— home base for our drumming circle. We soon had a weekly gig playing for a dance class and began to play bars and festivals around the Albany area.

Six months into my self-guided bliss project, I was doing four things I loved: learning to hunt, learning to distill, digging a grease pit, and drumming with friends. I was also working as a carpenter's assistant with Rod. I fantasized how these four glorified hobbies could support me financially. I tried putting them together in various combinations—a garage that served moonshine and venison while you waited? It was like trying to solve a defective Rubix Cube.

I was reminded of a powerful intuition I had had when I was six. My mother, exhausted from chasing after three small boys, would announce that it was "nap time" when she had finally had enough. Confined to my room for an hour, not remotely sleepy, I would look around my prison and contemplate how to crack the code of boredom. I somehow knew that if I could arrange all the objects already there into the right combination, I would never be bored again. Kind of like a perpetual motion machine, but for fun! Looking at what lay before me—a punching bag, a bear skin rug, LEGOs, my favorite book of Grimm's Tales, my four poster bed—I knew I had all the pieces I needed. I just couldn't figure out how to put them together.

I never banished my son, Kirby, to any obligatory "nap." He was learning to walk and he and I spent hours in the sandbox or on the living room floor playing with Tonka trucks. He loved construction equipment and had a talismanic toy backhoe that he carried with him everywhere and even slept with. I also shared my love of trains with him and we spent hours driving the back roads around Cambridge looking for freight trains and then following them for hours. We called this game "train chasing." It also gave me the chance to smoke and listen to grunge—Nirvana, Stone Temple Pilots, Soundgarden— on the radio, perfect for a small child.

In February of '95, my grandmother went into the hospital. She had been struggling for months with increasing memory loss and physical weakness, but this was different. She was at Dartmouth-Hitchcock, near where my father lived, and both of her other children, Joanna and Henry, were staying nearby, waiting for the end. I was in constant telephone contact with all three, but when I heard they had left her alone in the hospital for the night, I felt a pang. When I was alone and in danger as an infant, my grandmother stepped up. I had to be with her.

I drove the two hours to sit by her hospital bed, arriving a little after ten PM. The nurses told me the doctors could do no more for her. She was in a morphine-induced coma and it wouldn't be long before she stopped breathing. As I sat with her through the night, holding her hand, listening to her rasping breaths, she no longer looked like the woman I remembered. Her white hair was pulled back from her forehead, her long curved nose accentuated by her hollow cheeks. I was staring at an ancient Central American shaman.

In the morning, her three children joined us. I had to return home for work, but they promised to sit vigil until she passed. Shortly after I got home, word came that my grandmother had died. I felt heavy and light at the same time. This woman had been my "other mother," had always provided a safe haven, wise guidance through the storm. I wept at this loss. And I also had had the opportunity to give a little back, to be with her in her moment of need. A circle completed.

I had been out of the city almost a year. Rod, in addition to giving me my first job and hooking me up with a drumming circle, had also invited me to join a longstanding men's group he was part of. These guys were mostly professionals who commuted to Albany and had been meeting for over ten years. I was the youngest member. The "silver back" of the group, a sixty something named Jim, retired school administrator and dead ringer for my dad, questioned my project. "You have so many talents. You are so smart, a gifted writer, graduate of Yale Law. Why are you wasting your life?"

The question shook me. Suddenly, I was alone in a room with my father, struggling to account for myself. My dad had clear plans for me from the start. When I was small, he spent hours at the backboard with me during summers on Martha's Vineyard, trying, without luck, to teach me tennis because it would help me "get ahead." By the age of twelve, I knew I would be attending the same schools he did: Exeter and Harvard. This did not actually happen. I went to Andover and Oberlin; however, Andover was my grandfather's alma mater and I made up for Oberlin by attending Yale Law School. I was named George after all, like my father and his father and his father... I was the fifth George, all of us eldest sons. In college, the burden began to feel unbearable. The honors thesis I was working on in anthropology had to measure up to my grandfather's classic book on the Aztecs, my father's myriad publications in his chosen field of psychiatry.

The pressure to succeed drove me to law school, but halfway through I began to have second thoughts. I was sitting with my dad in his study, sharing these reservations, and told him I wanted to write fiction and poetry instead. His brow furrowed. "If you haven't been published by twenty-five," my father replied, " It probably isn't going to happen."

I had just turned twenty-six.

I set out to prove him wrong. Finished law school, started teaching, and got two poems and a short story published in my early thirties. But that became my main motivation: to get published. Now it wasn't just my father and grandfather looking over my shoulder, but dozens of faceless editors. It was too much. By moving to the country, I was starting over.

So when Jim challenged my bliss project, I was really hearing my father. Jim's words took me right back to when I was eighteen, after I had been caught smoking a cigarette in the graduation procession at Andover, back to my father's quiet judgment. "I have never been so ashamed of you. It was like watching a little boy holding his penis, showing it off at a dinner party."

That night, after the men's group meeting, I had a dream—I was out in the yard of the house where I lived when I was six, building a small wigwam out of twigs in the hopes that the sacred bear would live in it. I went back inside, and there, in the kitchen, on top of the fridge, was a statue of a golden bear. I knew it was for me.

I woke up and went out to the garage. At the center of the dirt floor was the partially dug grease pit, like an enormous grave. Hanging on the walls were several dried deerskins, souvenirs of my practice gutting sessions. Since a successful deer hunter's first action has to be to remove the entire digestive tract—trachea to anus—because it can spoil the meat if left in, I knew that performing this operation was just as important as finding and killing a deer. I also knew I would never get it right on the first try. Because there were so many road-killed deer in the area, I made a practice of gathering a couple every now and then and working on my surgical skills.

One morning, Nancy headed out the door to teach a poetry class. A minute later, she came back into the house, remarking acidly, "There is blood and hair all over the steering wheel." Traces of my previous evening's deer gathering run. She stood for a moment in the center of the room, hands on her hips, contemplating me. "You are not the tweedy fellow I fell for in college." But unlike with Jim or my dad, there was no judgment. She was simply making an accurate assessment.

I wasn't just gathering deer to test my surgical prowess. The topic of making our own drums had come up in my drumming circle. Although goat was the most common choice in Africa, why not use deerskins? The first plausible connection among my four bliss activities had arisen.

The day after Jim's question and my dream about bears, I saw the garage in a different way. Again, this was partly because of my dad. He was an avid hiker. Because my mom had no interest in the mountains, he took me with him as soon as I exhibited bipedal proficiency. It became a shared joy for us. He was a different person in the woods, a dog let out of the house. Once, when I was ten, I accompanied him to the summit of Mt. Lafayette in the White Mountains of New Hampshire. We looked out at the Pemigiwasset Wilderness, the largest uninhabited area I had ever seen, an endless ocean of spruce and pine, variegated greens

27

spreading out to fill my field of vision, pouring over the horizon. And then the kicker—"There are bears down there." My father's words sent shivers along my arms. I had just been shown an entirely different world—wild, immense, dangerous.

Rod, in addition to giving me my first job and hooking me up with two circles of men, had also become a spiritual advisor of sorts. He felt a deep kinship with Native Americans and knew alcohol was pointless, that only the "plant teachers" —marijuana, mushrooms, peyote— could be trusted. He had recently given me an actual bear skull, which I placed in a central spot on the wall of my garage.

Looking at the bear skull, the deer hides, the deepening hole in the floor—I knew that I was making a place for Bear to live, just as I had been in my dream. Everything I was doing, all these puzzle pieces which I could not make sense of yet, all had something to do with Bear.

More pieces fell into place soon after. On a clear night in July, my moonshining partner, Dave, and I were ready to run the still for the first time. It had been months in the making.

Our cooker was a stainless steel beer keg, stolen from a local liquor distributor. Attached to it was what looked like a top hat made out of copper. This in turn had two holes in it: one for the thermometer (to guide us to the sweet spot of 178 degrees), the other for the "worm," fifteen feet of half inch copper tube which ran out of the cooker and down through a large washtub full of cool water. Taking thirteen turns in the Appalachian tradition (learned from the Foxfire series of how-to books), the worm ended at the open lid of a ball jar. Here is where we would, with any luck, gather the Elixir, the aquavit, the water that burned—190 proof jet fuel.

The night was perfect—clear and dark, just how moonshiners have always liked it. We had little to fear from the ATF though. Washington County, NY, the state's biggest producer of illegal marijuana, was DEA territory. Just the same, distilling alcohol without federal authorization could cost you five years in jail and a minimum $10,000 fine. No need to draw attention to ourselves.

By night's end, we had produced enough "shine" for a couple of generous shots. And to test the liquid's flammability. To see the yellowish beer purified and transformed —distilled— into clear liquid after a couple of hours was remarkable enough. But then to see it set alight, its surface shimmering an unearthly blue, was some kind of magic. And that magic extended to the drinking of it. I had been taking shots for twenty years, but never like this. The alcohol content was so high that it burned like fire as it went down and produced an instantaneous euphoria, as if it truly were an elixir.

Afterwards we took a dip in the pond beyond the ramshackle barn, and gazed up at the stars, brighter and closer than I could remember. "There's the Big Dipper," said Dave, pointing to the eponymous cluster of seven stars. "Ursa Major, the Great Bear." We continued enjoying the starry night, chatting briefly about the drought we were in the middle of. "Worst in thirty years some farmers are saying," Dave said. "And no end in sight."

He headed home soon after and I went to bed. I was sleeping downstairs now, apart from Nancy. Although neither of us knew what was coming, this past year saw us drifting further and further apart. After having spent the previous six years walking to work together every day, sharing the same English department office and generous vacation schedule, our paths and passions were increasingly diverging. I had no interest in college politics and she felt queasy about the fact I was running an illicit distillery out of our home. Our fights had gotten louder and more frequent and made Kirby cry. Sleeping in separate beds, taking a little space, promised to ease the tension.

That night, I was awoken by the most frightening storm I had ever witnessed. My first awareness was water splattering on my face from a window three feet away. I then became aware of wind-stricken branches lashing the house, which was trembling beneath the storm's fury. My next thought went to the open windows of my truck. Because it hadn't rained for so long, I had lost the habit of closing them. But as I reached the front door, I hesitated. Was it safe to go outside? It only occurred to me later that I had never asked that question before.

The next day everyone was abuzz with the surprise storm. Not predicted by weather forecasters, it had contained a number of "micro bursts," small tornados which shattered acres of trees for miles. They lay in tangles along county roads, enough firewood for the next ten years. It also ended the drought.

Dave and I were having a different conversation. "Could it be? What are the odds? Impossible!" We knew that for ancient alchemists, the first distillers, getting a better buzz was not the point. They were engaged in sacred work. What occurred in the alembic, the Arabic word for the cooker/condenser unit, revealed what was going on within themselves. The microcosm *was* the macrocosm. The practitioner's purity, his degree of spiritual evolution, determined the outcome of his ritual experimentation. Water catching fire, lead becoming gold, was proof you were making progress on the spiritual path.

This concept extended past the individual. Once you had established the truth of your inner divinity, the power could be extended to the world around you. As below, so above. The microcosm of the alembic could determine outside events. The very stages of distillation—evaporation, condensation, precipitation—could be repeated in the larger world. A true alchemist, so the thinking went, could make it rain.

We knew we could not have affected the weather. But the sheer immensity of the coincidence staggered us. Such "magical thinking" is the precursor of science – look how Einstein's idea of relativity impacted Hiroshima. It can also lead to madness.

Three weeks after the storm, exactly one year into "doing what I loved," I finished the grease pit. It looked like I had dug a grave for Wilt Chamberlain and left room for a lot of his favorite stuff. Later that same day was the second occasion of "Camping with Men," the effort of me and several of my friends—Rod, Dave, Scott and John—the men from my drumming circle— to dream up an appropriate coming of age ceremony for Scott's thirteen year old stepson. An older friend had asked us, "Have any of you been initiated?" We were still wrestling with that question as we headed out to the woods. We didn't bring the stepson. We had no idea what to do for him.

Making that night even more full of import was the fact that we were going to take psilocybin, the hallucinogen first made famous by Richard Alpert and Timothy Leary. Taking it in its original mushroom form made it seem even more mysterious. It also terrified me. Twenty years before, at Andover, I had met a book called In Search of the Magic Mushroom. At 16, I was convinced it held the answers I was yearning for. I imagined the walls of my cinderblock dorm room dissolving, allowing me to step into Narnia. The best we could do at the time was LSD and it only took three tries for me to wind up in a really bad trip, convinced I was about to die from strychnine poisoning.

Now, in my mid-thirties, I had the opportunity to work with the very magic mushrooms I had longed for as a teenager, but this time I had wiser traveling companions. First and foremost was John, whose previous work in theatre and time in the Alaska wilderness made him our unofficial "shaman." With his dark hair and moustache, he reminded me of a young Omar Sharif. Just two years older than me, he knew to follow his bliss wholeheartedly in high school (hence his forays in theatre and to Alaska) and combined a director's intuition for group dynamics with a deep love and feel for the natural world. Before we ate the mushrooms, he led us in a ritual process of first sharing our deepest fears and our greatest hopes. He wanted us properly focused. My greatest fear was that I would never find my purpose and I longed to fill my life with joy.

Rod and I were cutting down a dead tree for firewood with a crosscut saw when the psilocybin started to kick in. The saw began to take on a life of its own, as if it were a roller coaster car picking up speed, carrying us with it. Putting the saw down and returning to the fire, I noticed someone had been at work carving the stones circled around it. Instead of rough pieces of schist and quartzite, they were now carved frogs and snakes in an Olmec or Toltec style. The bark of the spruce log I was sitting on was no longer layered in random patterns, but had arranged itself in the repeating geometry of Celtic or Viking art. Even the tree branches around me were no longer simply going this way and that, but moved as living creatures; a Chinese dragon rose behind me, about to take flight.

I saw that tribal art was not the work of primitive peoples who had yet to grasp the principles of perspective; it consisted of Polaroid-accurate snapshots of the "other" reality, the world that lay just behind the veil. The world I had been trying to get to since I first heard of Jack and the Beanstalk, read The Lion, the Witch and the Wardrobe.

Immediately, my rational mind kicked in. A sneering voice—it could have been Jim from my men's group or my dad—"That's just your mind on drugs." I could even see the egg frying in the pan, the image used in a recent anti-drug campaign. But a stronger voice was also speaking. "Pay attention. This is important."

John called to me. "Hey, come hold hands with me around this tree."

As our hands clasped around the oak, just barely reaching around its circumference, everything went into color. Instead of the dark silhouette of a tree, I was embracing a column of shimmering purple and green energy, writhing and alive with immense and effortless power. I could see that what normally looked like stationary patterns in bark were actually rippling waves of energy. "Damn!" I thought, "Trees really are alive!"

We awoke the next morning and returned to our ordinary lives. Driving home, though, I knew something important had happened, something huge. Nancy did not agree. She reminded me that I'd promised to accompany her on an expedition to the mall to get roller blades for her niece, a gift of gratitude for her babysitting Kirby.

Although the most intense effects of psilocybin are felt for four to six hours after taking it, its secondary effects can last several days. I had not yet learned this so I didn't realize I was still tripping. As the endless squat rectangles of the mall hove into view, I could see their true purpose: although filled with items you "needed" or "wanted," each store was actually a baited trap with a single purpose—to lure you in and suck as much money out of your pockets as possible before you returned to your senses. I vowed to be on guard.

Walking the carpeted hallways, I peered into each business with suspicion. And then we came to the WaldenBooks. I had grown up with immense respect for books. The walls of the houses I grew up in, of all my relatives and friends, were lined with books. All my most admired relatives had written books. Intelligent literacy was the benchmark of civilization as I knew it. However, in this store, even the book had been skillfully packaged, monetized, designed to seduce.

I stepped carefully around neatly piled stacks of cookbooks and books about angels, until I came to a tall bookcase. Even though it held hundreds of volumes, I saw only one: *The Way of the Shaman*, by Michael Harner. I reached for it without thinking.

Ever since I was a teenager, the word "shaman" held numinous power. My Aunt Joanna's husband, Ellis, the man I most admired, called himself a shaman. Of course, he was a "real Indian," part Lakota and Apache, so that was a career option for him. But not for me. As a northern European mutt, I could never be a shaman. No one ever told me this. I just knew it to be true.

The epigraph inside the cover grabbed my attention, words from an Inuit poem: *Everything that is, is alive!* I was suddenly back at the oak tree. Reading further, I found a description of how shamans often journeyed to the lower world, some even going so far as to dig a large hole in the earth floor of their houses. The grease pit.

The author continued to explain that shamans often worked with power animals, sometimes even shape shifting into them. The words of a Tlingit prayer followed: "I throw bear grease into the fire. Whu, bear! We are one!" The book was starting to enfold me.

Settling into a chair in the bookstore corner nook, I read that shamans were most often found in hunting/gathering societies, that the shaman was often seen as "Master of animals." the indispensable source of hunting medicine. The kind of man who always got a deer.

Shamans helped with other matters as well, such as healing or making rain. To do the latter they would conduct ceremonies which would replicate themselves in the larger world. "As above, so below..." A shaman could end a drought.

Finally, the book explained, while some shamans did use entheogens, Greek for "becoming divine within" (also referred to as "plant teachers"), such as peyote or psilocybin, their primary source of transport was the drum. The book even contained a reference section with recommendations for books on drum making.

In the car now, heading home, roller blades on the backseat, Michael Harner's *The Way of the Shaman* gripped in my hands, I experienced my entire life metamorphosing into a different form. I was reminded of my first visit to the Museum of Fine Arts in Boston, at thirteen, when I was standing just two feet away from Monet's Haystack at Sunset. Staring at what looked like a random spattering of yellows and greens, violets and orange, I could feel the jump to clarity as I took three steps back and a meadow and haystack appeared. And now, a random series of explorations came unexpectedly into focus: I was a shaman.

Following my bliss had taken me on a quantum leap out of everyday space and time into a realm way beyond the world I had been living in for thirty-six years. This wasn't just "doors opening where there were no doors." This was the Door. My new life had begun.

"Follow your bliss..." The words were my mantra. But there was a shadow side to this mandate as Jim had mentioned in our men's group. As I was sharing my breakthrough with the other men, Jim reminded me, "Absolutely. Doors do open when you follow your bliss. But following your bliss will also bring you up against all the fears which, before, kept you from doing what you longed to do."

A silence followed his pronouncement as we each digested this caveat to Joseph Campbell's call to joy. A shadow fell over the room. He wasn't just being a wet blanket, playing the conservative father to my ebullient child. There was deep truth here. If I was serious about following my bliss, I would need to enter some scary territory.

Chapter 3

The Shaman's Path

The first thing I ever wanted to be when I grew up was an Indian. I knew this from reading books. They were my sanctuary, my safe place, from the age of five. We were living on Calumet Farm in Kentucky, the legendary racing stable. It was 1964, the Vietnam war was just getting started and my dad was at risk of being drafted, so he joined the U.S. Public Health Service in order to have some say in his posting. He chose to work at their narcotics hospital in Lexington where he began his groundbreaking work on addiction. Because the hospital was run by the Public Health Service, a branch of the Navy, my dad went out the door each morning dressed as a military officer, not returning til evening. My school hours were brief so mostly my mom and I and my two-year-old brother, John rattled around the house, miles from the nearest neighbor.

My mother's oscillating moods took her from playful kindness to silent depression to rage without warning. Books were steadier companions and the worlds they conjured up surrounded me like a cocoon. At five, reading about American Indians (as they were called then), I was struck by the Eastern Woodland lifestyle; something about living in wigwams resonated deeply. So determined was I to join my new "family," that I decided to do everything in my power to become like them. The book said they lived off roots and berries. This sounded doable. There were plenty of roots in the backyard.

Going out with my new jack knife, my prize possession, I went to the base of a spruce tree, dug a little, and cut off some exposed roots. Back inside, I waited until my mom was in a distant part of the house. I can still remember staring at the oven control knob, precisely at eye level, and considering the enormous numbers embossed upon it: 100, 200, 300... 150 was as high as I dared go.

I placed the roots on a small aluminum pan and put the pan in the oven. Waiting for as long as I could stand, probably twenty or thirty seconds, I pulled the pan out of the oven and placed the roots on my favorite Peter Rabbit plate. I can still see the painted rabbits, wearing clothes, playing games.

I was starting to feel some doubt. Those hairy roots did not appear remotely appetizing. Nor were they even warm. But I was determined. Shaking a little salt and pepper on them to make them more like food, I took my fork and knife and started sawing away. I can still taste the bitter flavor, feel the woody toughness of tree root in my mouth. "This can't be right."

My first success in my quest to be an Indian came through magic. My mom had advised me always to wish on hay trucks, a common sight where we were living. "They're good luck, you know." So whenever I spotted a truck piled high with bales of hay, I wished fervently for an "Indian suit," a popular costume in those days, consisting of faux leather leggings and vest with your choice of tomahawk or bow and arrows, rubber-tipped and manufactured in Japan.

Imagine my amazement when, under the Christmas tree that year, was an authentic Indian suit! Vest, leggings, bow and three arrows tipped with small rubber suction cups. How could my mother have known?

From then on, although I now knew I would never actually be an Indian, anything to do with Indians caught my attention.

This fascination had a brief setback when, at age eight, I read a children's biography of George Armstrong Custer. In the final scene, when the "red savages" close in on the unfairly outnumbered hero, I burst into tears. Were Indians bad?

Two years later, however, I saw *Little Big Man*, the groundbreaking film which revealed Custer's blood lust in a sharp light and I wept again. But this time, my tears contained outrage. I had been lied to!

That same year, I met Ellis, who had married my father's sister twenty years earlier when she was sixteen. He was a "real Indian." Native blood ran in his veins. Although he had been an aspiring poet in Greenwich Village in 1949 when my aunt met him, Ellis was a loving husband and a steadying influence on his sometimes impulsive wife. Equally important to my Grandmother Sue, Ellis was also a gifted mentor of troubled young men.

My career as a juvenile delinquent had yet to begin, but my grandmother sensed I was heading for trouble. I fought chronically with my younger brother, John, and was showing early signs of depression. She was taking no chances. She summoned Ellis from Michigan, where he and Joanna lived, and arranged for us to meet.

And so began a twenty-year relationship that saved my life. When I first met Ellis, he recalled later, he had no idea what to do with me. "Sue said, 'He needs you,'" Ellis remembered, "So I did what seemed like a good idea at the time." This involved teaching me to play the game, "The Devil Decides," a classic time waster for diner rats: you take a water glass, put a napkin on top, held tight with a rubber band, and place a dime at the center. The two combatants then take turns burning holes in the napkin with a cigarette until the dime falls. We played this game many times on the floor of my grandmother's sunporch. The perfect activity for a ten-year-old headed for trouble.

I loved it. And so began the endless conversations that would guide me for the next two decades. First, we talked of buried treasure and lost caches, waiting to be found. Gradually, we moved to dreams and the hero's journey. By this time, he and my aunt had moved east to our family farm in Connecticut.

Ellis grew up poor in rural Missouri in the twenties and was a sickly child. He remembered his mother's friends saying she would be "burying young bones" when they though he couldn't hear. He had a hunch back, a bad heart, and permanent physical damage from his father's abuse. Joanna was as much his nurse as his wife. Just the same, he was an extraordinary teacher. He never went to college but was probably the best read man I ever met. He also truly had a gift with troubled young men. In Michigan, he ran what he called the "Orchard Academy," an informal school for young car thieves who had been expelled from the Grand Ledge high school. Even though these young men had been headed for prison, Ellis got them reading Shakespeare and Plato and many of them went on to become civic leaders.

When Ellis taught, it wasn't like being with a "teacher" in the usual sense of the word. He made you feel like he had known Shakespeare personally, had actually hung out with Plato. He had a novelist's ear for dialogue and eye for setting but he never wrote fiction. He created worlds out of words for young men like me to inhabit.

His life was out of a book: he had ridden the rails in in his teens and served in the army after the war in China and Korea. In Greenwich Village, he would watch his neighbor, Jackson Pollack, paint. He had served drinks to Lucky Luciano and dined with Carl Jung. He had even been initiated into the Native American Peyote Church. He called himself a "shaman" and we did not doubt him.

Living in Connecticut, Ellis was like Prospero in The Tempest, his favorite play. The forty-acre farm was his island. He even nicknamed me Ariel after the magician's assistant (and bound servant). My brother, John, and I became his new students and gradually our best friends were drawn in as well, my Andover roommate, "Chief," and John's school chum, Seb.

We were all misfits. Neither my brother, John, nor I ever felt comfortable in our inherited lives as Mayflower descendants, children of Boston "Brahmins." We hated tennis and saw our private school teachers as oppressors. Likewise, Chief, born as John Evans, was an African-American who could not play basketball, no matter how many hours his pastor put in with him under the basket behind the church, trying to fill in for Chief's father, who died when he was one. Chief's mother, the only daughter of African-Americans who fled north for factory jobs during World War Two, saw her role as helping Chief continue this northern ascent. She enrolled him in private school early and I'd met him at Andover. She confided in me once that she never wanted her son "to feel like he was black."

Seb, the son of a scientist and an artist, felt as out of place in wealthy suburban Belmont as any of us did in our native habitats. His escape was the woods near his home where he spent the bulk of his time after school attempting to recreate a stone age life style, learning to build lean-to's out of dead fall and fashioning his own bows and arrows out of natural materials. When Ellis first met him, even though Seb was then a successful student at Wesleyan, he told me later that the young man was "almost feral." He meant it as a compliment.

I started spending my summers with my Aunt Joanna and Uncle Ellis after tenth grade, in 1975, and soon my brother did, too. Chief and Seb started joining us on weekends after we were all at college and the four of us continued to meet regularly with Ellis for the next ten years. He became our "shaman" and helped us create ceremonies and guided us on quests. No longer were we just confused adolescents; we were aspiring heroes studying under Chiron the wise Centaur and "wounded healer," teacher of Ajax, Theseus, Achilles. He helped us recognize the journey each of us was on—how our dilemmas were no different than those of the heroes who came before us. He taught us how to read our dreams and see the mythical elements in our struggles, their archetypal implications.

Ellis remained my lodestar until I was thirty, when we had a falling out. Ever since I first connected with him at ten, I took everything he said as gospel, followed his every instruction to the letter. This worked well during adolescence. He provided a structure and sense of meaning that I desperately needed. As I got into my late twenties, I began to challenge his ideas and resisted the role of disciple. He demanded complete obedience. I refused. We never came to a resolution and my drinking really took off.

I was a "masterless ronin," a warrior without guidance, and my compass swung with my desires. It was just a year after Ellis's death from emphysema, when I was thirty-five, that I made the decision to move to the country and do "what I loved." Meeting Michael Harner's book broke the spell of my own internalized bias; white men could, in fact, drum. It was possible for me to go after my dream job.

My first step on this new path was to call the number in the back of Harner's book. Although it was no longer in service, the recording provided a new one and an address. I put my check in the mail and waited for what I hoped would be the key to a new life: a cassette tape of a shamanic drumming journey.

Although many in the west are captivated by the shamanic use of entheogens, shamans often used a drum to travel to the invisible worlds. Especially in northern latitudes, the one-sided frame drum, eighteen to twenty-four inches in diameter, is the shaman's preferred mode of transport. Called the tom-tom on the Plains, the bodhran in Ireland, used by the Sami people in northern Scandinavian and by shamans in Siberia, this type of drum is thousands of years old, time-tested.

41

More recently, western scientists using an EEG discovered an explanation for this choice. The vibrations of this type of frame drum are at a frequency close to that of brain waves when we are in the Alpha or REM state, the frequency of dreaming. After listening to the sound of such a drum, our brain waves entrain with this frequency, putting us into a waking dream state. In addition, left brain activity subsides and right brain activity is stimulated. Essentially, listening to the drum helps us to "think" like a shaman. I call it "right brain rehab."

While at the Esalen Instutute in the 1960's, anthropologist, Michael Harner, and psychiatrist, Stanislav Grof, were seeking a way to replicate the effects of hallucinogens without using drugs. They found that drumming could produce a similar yet less intense effect. The listener could leave the experience by opening his eyes. The tape I had ordered was a fruit of this discovery.

For Grof, LSD was the hallucinogen which had inspired his quest for a sonic alternative. For Harner, it had been ayahuasca. Back in the 1950's, when it was virtually unknown in the west, ayahuasca changed the course of Michael Harner's life. He was a young, ambitious anthropologist, studying the Shuar people in eastern Ecuador. At the time, he had no interest in hallucinogens; he was trying to make his bones studying a tribe about which almost nothing was known. The Shuar had driven the Spanish out of their territory permanently in 1599—the only indigenous tribe known to have inflicted such a defeat on a colonizing power. Other stone age tribes may have driven metal-working, gun-wielding invaders out for a while, but, in the case of the Shuar, the Spanish never came back.

Another reason no one bothered them was their tradition of "shrinking heads"—cutting the heads off enemies, removing the skull, and shrinking the remaining face and scalp to wear as adornment. Better to leave these ayahuasca-drinking, head-hunting maniacs alone. In fact, at that time, no one called them the Shuar. They were known as the Jivaro, the "ferocious people." So when Michael hiked down the eastern slopes of the Andes into the upper Amazon basin to study these people, no one was sure he would actually come back.

However, according to Harner, when the Shuar weren't out hunting heads, they were kind and gentle. The men often played with their children and cried easily. The place where he found them implacable was when he inquired about their spiritual beliefs. They refused to tell him anything. Finally, one man explained their hesitance. "Unless you drink *natema* (the Shuar word for ayahuasca), you could not to understand what we are talking about."

And that settled it. The anthropological principle of "participant observation" required Harner to drink the brew if he were to be able to complete his ethnography. He had no idea what he was getting into. Before the ceremony was over, he was convinced they had intentionally poisoned him and that he was going to die. Calling out for the antidote, he was swept into an overwhelming hallucination where beings from another world explained that, because he was about to die, they were going to share some secrets about human destiny that the living are forbidden to know.

He awoke to sunlight streaming through the jungle canopy, macaws crying above, smoke from a cooking fire, the laughter of children. He was still alive. When he had pulled himself together sufficiently to converse, he asked to be taken to the village shaman where, through a translator, he poured out his remarkable experience.

The man was not impressed. Interrupting Harner before he was halfway though, he finished the story himself, frequently adding details. For Harner, it was as if he had made his first visit to a strange town, mentioned a couple of landmarks, and this long time native was filling in the gaps. For the shaman, Harner's experience was not a hallucination, but a first visit to a world with a known topography, whose inhabitants often treated new visitors this way.

The old man then said, "Few are shown so much on their first journey. You have the potential to be a great shaman. You should stay with us. I will teach you."

I would have given an eye for such an opportunity. But in 1957, it would have been professional suicide. Harner came back to America and wrote his dissertation. However, something about the old shaman's offer wouldn't leave him alone. In 1963, he returned to the Shuar and completed his shamanic training. Now it was even harder to come back to the United States.

Harner became a respected healer in the tribe, but in the United States, he could not share his experiences with anyone. Who would understand? It was 1963. Men still wore hats and J. Edgar Hoover was the final arbiter of what was true and good. However, Harner was a man with immense passion and self-confidence. Even though he had "run out of his ayahuasca supply," as he would later joke, he knew there were native peoples in North America who were shamans. How did they get to the other realms?

Studying with the Lakota and the Salish and in, Northern Europe, with the Sami people, Harner learned that the drum was their vehicle to altered consciousness. Perhaps not as dramatic as ayahuasca (I liken the difference to that between Nirvana unplugged and the same band doing a fully amplified live show), the drum took you to the same place. And that's what he taught for the next fifty years.

The day the cassette arrived, I popped it into my Walkman and climbed down into my recently dug grease pit, pulling the wooden cover down behind me. The pit could serve other purposes than being a "poor man's lift." Following Harner's directions to first visualize a place in nature and then to use that location as my "entry point" to the Lower World, I closed my eyes and immediately launched into the following experience:

44

I am in the hole, dropping, dropping, until I am in the forest where we took the psilocybin. It is night. I hear sounds, heard them as I was dropping. There are bears everywhere and I am a bear. We are dancing to the drum.

I hear low growls. I am in the center of a circle of four bears. We dance through the woods, into a huge clearing thronged with bears dancing. I dance, my claws huge, my jaws immense. Then the other bears are gone.

I am alone. I am in the cliff cave, the secret spot. I float out over the stream, high above the woods. The land undulates gently below me. I float up and up. I am Ursa Major, the Great Bear, outstretched over the earth, embracing the earth, playing with it like the bears at the zoo play with their bowling ball and beer keg. I am the stars that light the way north, that pointed slaves to freedom.

I float and spin in space. The darkness of the universe is hard and cold against my back. It is an immense cave. The universe is a vast cave. I emerge into light, day, brightness. There is an Indian encampment, Plains tribe, Sioux? The humming overtones of the drum become the voice of an old man, a shaman, singing. I peel off my bear skin and am embraced by a beautiful woman. The shaman's daughter.

We make love in her teepee. I can feel the buffalo skins we lie upon. I travel inside her. I am in a huge dark cave, a river, like tree branches, her Fallopian tubes. I am born out of her and emerge as a bear again, to float back up into the sky, Ursa Major once more.

The drum calls the return and I descend, float back over the valley, to the cliff, the clearing, the stream, back up the tunnel to the grease pit.

I lie on its floor. I feel exalted, ecstatic, stunned, stoned. I can barely pick myself up. I climb out of the pit with difficulty. What the hell just happened? I have no context to put it in. It won't be for another fifteen years that I will realize I have just been shown the birth and death of my second marriage, to a woman I haven't yet met.

As Jim had pointed out in men's group, one of the biggest obstacles to following your bliss is fear. This had been the case for me with chronic depression showing up as fear's representative. For how many years had depression stalked me as I made excuses for not doing what I really wanted to? One striking example was my decision to go to law school, the low point of my life as a student. The parts of me that depression preyed on— where I felt shame, like a loser, inadequate— all spoke out in favor of law school. Going to a top law school looked like the antidote for my self-loathing. The power and prestige promised by the degree would provide the armor my low self-esteem required, could win my father's approval.

Jim was right. My fears had long prevented me from following my bliss. But there was something more in his words, a warning. It wasn't just that our fears kept us from our bliss; pursuing what lights us up has consequences as well.

A little less than a year had passed since my mushroom experience. I had read Michael Harner's book, obtained a drumming cassette to use for shamanic journeying, and, thanks to a small inheritance from my grandmother, had taken several of his workshops, including a two week intensive at Esalen in Big Sur, which Harner taught with Sandra Ingerman. Spending twelve days in that otherworldly setting, journeying many times every day with fifty other people, puts you into a state that is hard to describe. The realms usually only accessed in dreams or with hallucinogens became your waking reality, constantly reinforced by repeated drumming sessions and a whole community who was living in that same reality as well. Anything seems possible!

Michael Harner later confided to me, "When we first started doing this program, it was a month long. But we found nobody could go back to their lives. They were walking out of their jobs, their marriages. It was just too disruptive." He paused, looking out over the Pacific with a faint smile. "So we settled on two weeks."

And he was right. It was hard to go back. My first day with my now almost three-year old son saw me drifting in and out of reverie, reliving journeys, conversations from the previous two weeks. "That's not a story, Dad!" he impatiently interrupted, as my bedtime story drifted into murmurings about my power animal.

There was also a bigger disruptor. I had fallen in love at Esalen. We had gone deep, had passionate sex, sworn fidelity. "You look like you just got married," Chief said to me when I showed him a picture of Lisa and me taken on the last day of the program.

We exchanged letters, made furtive phone calls. The fact she lived in LA was a challenge, but she was all I could think about. I made no effort to conceal the letters she sent me, leaving them in a pile on my desk. Nancy and I were pretty alienated by now. The fact I was getting messages from trees completely wigged her out. She felt me slipping away and I was eager for change. Her finding the letters was my unconscious hope. It took a couple of months for her to notice them.

This event occurred the day I quit smoking. I came home one afternoon and Nancy met me at the door, brandishing the letters. She was furious. What was I thinking? The truth was all I was thinking about was how badly I wanted a cigarette. The deeper meaning of giving up an addiction was lost on me. I felt blindsided. Here I was trying to do this "good" thing—stop smoking-- and I was getting blasted for being bad. I was deeply in love with Lisa, but I was in upstate New York, living in a house I owned with my wife and three-year old son. Lisa was a world away. I cut my losses without a fight and promised Nancy I'd break it off.

I remember driving my truck down Route 22 in the days that followed— going to work, to the market, to pick Kirby up from a baby sitter— stiff arming the steering wheel with one hand, head cocked to the side, jaw clenched. I felt like a stallion confined to a stall. No matter how hard I kicked, whinnied or bit, this was my life.

One day, I was sitting in the sandbox with Kirby as he played in the dirt with his little toy backhoe. He still carried it everywhere, often holding it out in front of him as he walked, as if for protection. It was his talisman, his power object.

While he dug in the dirt with his "heavy equipment," I considered that his single-minded focus was like that of a Zen master who could "see the world in a grain of sand."

As I reflected on this parallel, Kirby spun around with the backhoe in his hand and gouged me in the forehead. Such behavior was completely unlike him. He was a very gentle being. As I began to feel a warm trickle on my face, Kirby drew his finger along my nose to catch the blood. Putting his now bloody finger into his mouth, he said, "Mmm! Tasty food, Dad!"

Before I could say a word, he turned away and was once again digging in the ground as if nothing had happened. I was stunned. I had a flash of the Zen master coming upon a dozing student, striking him hard with a bamboo rod to bring the younger man back into the moment. And there was also something much more primitive going on—the cutting, the blood, Kirby's utter matter-of-factness, reminded me of some kind of shamanic initiation. Who was this kid?

This wasn't the first time Kirby had schooled me. At his birth, a year before I started to fully follow my bliss, I had been in the delivery room when the midwife announced he was crowning and invited me to put my hand on his head. As I placed my palm on his tiny skull, the midwife instructed me to hold on tight. Kirby's wet head, lightly feathered with hair, pushed into my hand. "Tight!" the midwife commanded.

And then his head was filling my hand, his whole body pouring into my cupped palms and I was holding him. His face was blue and there were reddish bubbles forming on his lips. His nose was flattened and his brow sloped back in a disturbing way. I had a sudden recollection of the movie, *Total Recall*, where the prophet and leader of the Mars uprising isn't an actual man, but a sort of homunculus that emerges from time to time out of another character's belly.

What I was holding in my hands was not entirely human, not from Earth. And he was my son! And he was alive! The joy at beholding my first child, the incredible relief that he had survived this bloody ordeal overwhelmed me. I burst into tears. Holding his tiny warm body very close, I sobbed and sobbed. I have never felt happier or more relieved.

I felt how extraordinarily thin and delicate the veil between life and death is. In daily life, we have almost no awareness of this constant fragility. But here, in the birthing room, the curtain had been drawn back for a moment, revealing the presence of life and death as our constant and close companions. The energy of this sudden awareness was extraordinary.

That afternoon, in the dirt with Kirby, watching him move his tiny backhoe through the earth, the blood still sticky on my forehead, I realized shamans, like midwives, deliver not babies but the human soul. They both facilitate access to the deepest mysteries, the most powerful energies human beings are capable of experiencing. And some of these are hard to survive.

A couple of months after confronting me about my affair with Lisa, Nancy asked, "So, were there any others?" I felt a little sick. Yeah, there were others. None as serious as Lisa, but there had been a lot of sex. I had in fact been following my deepest "bliss" ever since Joseph Campbell confirmed my unspoken prayer in 1988. At that point, six years into my first marriage, monogamy felt like a trap. I knew I was missing out on important things. I had to explore what sex would be like with someone other than my wife. Increasingly since then, I had been having one-night stands whenever the opportunity permitted.

Until meeting Lisa at Esalen, the idea of a full-on double life—wife in one lane, lover in the other— felt like too massive a deception. My conscience, such as it was, couldn't take that lie. However, brief encounters without emotional connection felt ok. This wasn't cheating. Just a little harmless exploration.

The fact is, if we are going to talk about bliss, we are going to have to talk about sex. What is the most fantastic, most amazing thing you have ever felt? Orgasm was designed to be the ultimate motivator. Whatever reason we may think we have for existing, nature has one purpose: multiply!

One of the perks of having been a musician was a lot of female attention. Nancy didn't come to all my gigs and I took advantage of her absence. In fact, I had taken advantage of her absence whenever possible starting when she had gone to a six month writer's residency a few years earlier. She was doing what she wanted to do and leaving me alone. Wasn't I entitled to do what I wanted?

This thinking, especially when I was drinking, was irresistible. I wasn't yet familiar with the twelve-step definition of an alcoholic: "Instant asshole. Just add alcohol." But it fit perfectly. Prior to Lisa, I had slept with over a dozen women.

I hesitated, filled with fear of the consequences of honesty and shame at what I had done. But Nancy was insistent. "Tell me, " she said, "I have to know."

As I got into the double digits (nothing "serious," one night stands, make out sessions, "almosts"), I looked up and met her eyes. Nancy wasn't crying. She was stunned. Her expression mirrored the magnitude of my betrayal: Here was a person who was supposed to be her best friend, who was the father of her child, and he had treated her worse than anyone else in her life. She had done nothing to me and I was stabbing her in the heart. Again and again and again.

I felt like I was drowning. Waves of remorse and horror swept over me. There was the decent guy I had thought I was and now there was this man. I could see him reflected in Nancy's eyes, something out of a nightmare. I was Dr. Jekyll looking at the horrifying handiwork of Mr. Hyde and realizing I had done it. I had taken my wife's trust and used it to camouflage my own cruel behavior.

There was nothing solid under my feet, nothing to hold on to. And then, in that terrible moment, a thought surfaced in my mind like a life ring thrown from a nearby ship— "I was drinking every time I cheated on her." Not drunk every time, but at least a couple of drinks in. If I hadn't been drinking, none of those infidelities would have occurred. I knew this because none ever had.

This did not absolve me. It in no way excused my behavior. It didn't help Nancy much. But this realization showed a way forward, a path of hope: I might not be able to change what I had done, but I could stop drinking. It took another year before I could accept that I was actually an alcoholic, get into a twelve-step program, but this was watershed moment. I may have wrecked my marriage, but I knew what I needed to do.

Chapter 4

Vision Quest

A few weeks after that terrible day, I made the commitment to do my first vision quest. This decision, of course, began with a journey. A friend of mine who had already completed Michael Harner's three-year shamanic training program (a much bigger commitment than the five and ten-day workshops I had already taken and something I aspired to), told me about a series of journeys developed by one of Michael's top teachers, Christina Stack. The first was to journey to the moment before one's soul incarnated and ask it what its purpose was.

This pretty much nailed my number one question: what was my purpose? Not being able to figure this out often metastasized into deep depression. When I was lucky, these moods would pass. When I wasn't, they could drag me into contemplating suicide. Getting an answer to this question was not idle speculation.

I wasn't using my grease pit much to work on cars, but it was a fantastic spot for entering what Harner called "nonordinary reality." Going down the steps I built, pulling the wood panels over the top, I had already entered a different world. Down here, on the damp concrete, unable to see my hand in front of my face, I was in a sacred cave. Repeating my intention— What was my soul's purpose in the moment before I incarnated?—I put my Walkman on.

The journey began dramatically.

I was in Vietnam, badly wounded. Both legs had been struck by bullets and I was unable to walk. Michael Harner and Sandra Ingerman were on either side of me, arms around me, half carrying me, half dragging me out of the jungle to the waiting medevac.

Once airborne, they lifted me up and brought me over to the open hatch door to look out at the scenery. Instead of Vietnam, I saw the Badlands of South Dakota, dry and desolate, punctuated by spires of red and yellow sandstone. Before I could say anything, Michael and Sandra threw me out the door. I was falling through space, my body spinning, until it was caught, punctured by one of the sandstone spires.

I continued to fall, down, down, into the earth, through endless layers of rock, until I landed in a dark cave. There was a fire burning, and across from it, an ancient blind Lakota man—my Spirit teacher—with long white braids decorated with turquoise and bone, his eyes blank and sightless. He was chuckling at my predicament. And as he did, he kept repeating the same words over and over: "Four days and four nights, no food, no water. Four days and four nights. No food and no water..."

That was all he would say about my purpose. If I wanted to know more, I would have to go on a vision quest.

The term, "vision quest," is a Western one, used to describe the ancient Plains tribes' tradition by anthropologists who were reminded of stories of King Arthur and the Grail. Here, however, the search was not for a mythical cup, but a vision.

The Lakota call this ceremony the Hanbleceya, literally "crying for a vision," and the participants often weep as they go out "onto the mountain:" "I am poor, weak, helpless. My people are desperate. They are starving. Please, Grandfathers, give me a vision to feed my people."

It is a rite of great humility, performed by every generation since ancient times, and the survival of the People depends upon it.

In many ways, this tradition describes the origin of all the world's religions. Moses, Buddha, Jesus, Mohammad—each one went alone into the desert or the forest or the mountain, praying, crying desperately, for some scrap of wisdom to help his people. The fruits of these prayers continue to guide and nourish billions of people. But members of the Plains tribes don't believe God has stopped speaking.

Traditionally, an initiate is guided by a medicine man or woman, a shaman. The great Lakota medicine man, Black Elk, warned, in The Sacred Pipe; Black Elk's Account of the Seven Rites of the Oglala, that for a person to go unaided into the wilderness can be very dangerous.

The location of my quest would be where I had taken mushrooms the year before. The same four men who were with me then— Rod, Dave, John and Scott— agreed to be my sponsors and guardians.

Rod had never been distracted by the lure of status and prestige, recognizing early his kinship with Native peoples and his desire to avoid the "white man's world" as much as possible. He already knew who his power animal was—the buffalo. He already knew alcohol was a waste of time and that the "plant teachers" were infinitely superior guides. He knew all the trees that grew in the forest and made his living turning locally sourced wood into furniture and art.

During the months after we took mushrooms, the two of us created a circle twenty feet across with eight-foot lengths of the pine tree we cut down, each set into the earth, like a ring of standing stones. Within the circle, we placed special stones, rocks with faces or glimmering with quartz. We were creating a medicine wheel, a mandala, an ancient microcosmic representation of the universe. This would be the setting for my vision quest.

I made the mistake of telling a few people about my plans. When I mentioned that I planned to spend four days in the woods alone, without food or water, seeking a vision, everyone looked at me as if I were cracked.

"You'll die!"

"My doctor says you will be hallucinating within two days."

"Why would you want to do that?"

Nancy told me I was running away.

Despite all this good advice, I was excited.

I had no idea what I was in for.

Although I did not have an embodied shaman to guide me, I did have a group of men to watch over me. They wouldn't physically accompany me, but they agreed to pray for me while I was gone, to light candles at night, and meet me immediately upon completion of the quest.

The first thing you have to get used to on a vision quest is not hunger or thirst or loneliness or fear. It's boredom. Our society has very little tolerance for inactivity. Ask people how they are doing. How many times is their answer, "Busy"?

We rarely permit ourselves to simply sit and be. There is always something to do. This was in a time before cell phones, but I had absolutely no experience with sitting under a tree with nothing to do for a hundred hours. And the rules of vision quest are very specific: you mark out a sacred space, the smaller the better, and you stay there. No going for walks or running errands. No books. No distractions. Praying and singing are the only permitted activities.

Within half an hour of entering the circle of upright logs, I felt restless.

When I was a boy, I was the kid with the tapping foot, the one who couldn't keep still. The kid getting in trouble. Today, I'd have been diagnosed with ADHD. Sitting quietly and doing nothing was not in my wheelhouse. This was one reason I found shamanic journeying so appealing. It's a spiritual modality for the hyperactive. Drums, power objects, altars, compelling images, instructions to follow, gear to obtain. Things to do. Journey on it! Splendid!

But alone in the woods, I ran up against the limits of available distractions pretty quickly. For a while, I admired the log circle Rod and I had built. To keep the querent focused, tradition requires he remain in a small area. My vision circle was constructed from seven logs, each set in the ground a few feet apart and standing as tall as a man. These seven pillars, plus a single living tree, stood in the eight points of a compass rose, a medicine wheel. For the next four days, I would walk clockwise— sunwise— around the inside of this circle, praying for my purpose to be revealed.

I wasn't permitted a watch. I had no idea how much time had passed. It felt like I was trapped in eternity. I remembered all the instructions for meditation I had read over the years: watch your thoughts, how they are like clouds, slowly taking form and disappearing one by one…. This was why I had never taken up meditation. It sounded like torture.

It was the perfect description of a vision quest. The boredom that immediately filled my attention to the horizon slowly contracted and was replaced by hunger. I found myself watching planes moving slowly above me and wishing they would throw down one of those meals they used to serve. Then, as the plane faded, so did the hunger, only to be replaced by thirst.

This excerpt is taken from notes written right after my return:

Late in the afternoon of the first day, dozens of birds suddenly appear, several species, all in pairs, chasing each other through the leaves in the forest canopy, singing and hollering, all around me—wrens, robins, jays, woodpeckers, warblers. It is as if they are engaged in some kind of game. After they go, I am struck by how much the leaves of trees are like birds, fluttering, whispering, moving where the air takes them, so light and far from earth. And then the trees, still, silent, rooted, holding space for all this busyness. Strange to think that one being—tree—can be so at home with so many different kinds of beings; birds living among their branches, stones among their roots.

I realized I had never before seen so many different birds at once. And, every afternoon, I eagerly awaited this air show. But I saw no more birds. What did it mean? As Black Elk observed, your vision can come from just a glimpse of a particular animal. Pay close attention to everything!

Black Elk also cautioned in The Sacred Pipe that you should never undertake a hanbleceya except under the supervision of a medicine man. Otherwise, he warned, you are in great danger. He even speaks of being attacked by a "great black snake." I wasn't too worried about that. But I did feel alone.

It wasn't until after I had gotten back and checked in with all my supporters, friends I had asked to pray for me, that one of them told me an astonishing story. "Chief," his nickname since childhood, had been my best friend since tenth grade. We had roomed together at Andover and Ellis had mentored both of us. However, whereas I had always been the "problem child," getting in trouble in prep school, taking time off from college and law school, he had always been focused and clear. He went to work at IBM after graduating from Brown and getting a masters at Princeton. He was still there fifteen years later.

While I was out in the woods starving myself, he was on a business trip to Cleveland. After my quest, we reviewed our experiences of the four days and discovered that, while I was watching those birds on my first afternoon, he was driving up Interstate 77 on the way to a client when he felt a strong urge to pull over. Parked in the breakdown lane, he closed his eyes and was overwhelmed by a vision of winged demons. On impulse, he took out an imaginary sword, did battle with these creatures, cutting and hacking and fighting them off. Then, as abruptly as it began, the vision ceased. He opened his eyes, put the rental into drive, and continued on his way to the client.

He had no other "visions" while I was out. Shivers went through me when he shared his account. I had not yet told him anything about my experience. Was it possible that what I had seen as songbirds had been something else? Was this the kind of experience Black Elk had warned about? Chief had my back.

By the third day of my quest, there was a rhythm. After I awoke at the foot of a small maple, the only living tree in the circle of logs Rod and I had made, hunger came, only a twinge at first on the horizon of awareness, growing slowly until it became all I could think about, tearing at my stomach, and then, slowly, subsided and disappeared. Then thirst would come. Then loneliness. Then grief. Then boredom. Then these beautiful expanses of complete peace. And then hunger would approach again.

However, aside from this internal parade of thoughts and sensations, nothing seemed to be happening. So, on the third day, when a shaft of sunlight cut through the forest canopy and struck a nearby tree, I was transfixed. The abrupt brilliance amongst endless shade held my attention for minutes, until it, too, slid away. As I looked longingly at the spot on the tree's trunk where the sun had so deliciously embraced it, I was struck to see a dragonfly land there. I had never seen one so deep in the woods. Their preferred hunting ground is in meadows or by lakes or ponds, where mosquitos, their favorite prey, are most plentiful. The large insect lingered for what felt like minutes until it, too, floated off into the gloom.

It wasn't until after my quest that I learned about the remarkable lives of dragonflies. They first live, often for over a year, as water creatures in the nymph or naiad stage, lovely names belying their actual existence as ferocious predators with pincers and disturbingly large eyes (Think "bug-eyed"). They spend this aquatic phase lurking in the mud at the bottom of ponds, feeding surreptitiously on other bugs and even small fish. When they feel threatened, they rarely stand and fight, preferring to shoot water out of their rectums, propelling themselves quickly out of harm's way and leaving a large muddy cloud to hide their trail.

After a year or two of this furtive existence, the dragonfly nymph crawls up a reed stem, out of its familiar darkness, into the light and air, breathing through a rectal gill as its back slowly splits open to allow the dragonfly hidden inside to emerge. Once free of the husk of its old body, the newly hatched dragonfly clings helplessly for hours, completely exposed, suspended between worlds, as it takes its first breaths, as its heart slowly pumps blood into the myriad vessels in its wings. Only then can it take its first flight out into the open air, seeking its new food. A single dragonfly will eat over a hundred mosquitos daily.

After my vision quest, Aunt Joanna told me that for many believers, the dragonfly is a symbol of the risen Christ, both because of its metamorphosis and its body shape, much like a double armed cross. What it made me think of was getting sober—from sneaking around in the dark, furtively feeding, to being driven into the light to become profoundly useful to the whole community.

During my isolation, though, I knew none of this. What was eating at me, burning inside, was my lack of a clear sense of purpose. What was I supposed to do with my life?

I sat in the space left by this question, stuck, frustrated, wanting to shake an answer out of the trees around me, smash some guidance out of the stones at my feet. My life depended on getting an answer.

Somewhere out of this confused silence, words floated to the surface of my mind (again taken from the notes I made right after my return):

Every thing's purpose is contained within it.

I continue my slow walk around the vision circle. More clarity emerges.

Each being's purpose is inherent; it simply needs to be allowed to emerge of its own accord. The maple tree next to me does not torment itself with questions of purpose. It just <u>be's</u> a tree. The stone under my feet experiences no uncertainty. It simply <u>be's</u> a stone. All we have to do is Be.   Just leave ourselves alone and trust that what lies within us will come together and rise up of its own nature.

Be!

It is this simple. Simply

Be!

At that instant, the silence is split by the scream of a cicada, cutting the air like the whine of a circular saw.

Beeeeeeeeeeeeeee!

The high-pitched sound blasts my epiphany through the forest.   A clarion call of absolute certainty, it goes through my doubt, my clouded vision, like a hot knife through butter. I have never felt clearer, never felt lighter, and it is all so obvious:

  Everything, everywhere is absolutely perfect <u>just as it is</u>. No matter how much apparent chaos or torment or pain. It is all perfect. This is exactly how it should Be at this moment.

Everything stopped. The perfect peace of all creation was completely obvious, inarguable. Even the title of a book I had been reading, Be Here Now, Ram Dass's account of meeting his guru, was too wordy. There was no need for Here or Now.   The simple word, Be, said everything.

There was no need for action or laborious quests. You did not need to "crawl on your hands and knees through the desert for hundreds of miles." All I needed to do was Be. My purpose was inside, burning its own way to the surface, as effortlessly and naturally as the sun comes out of the eastern ocean, as the leaves bud on the maples around me each spring.

I had never in my entire life felt such joy, such peace, such an overwhelming sense of relief. For the next several hours, I floated on the endless Beeeeeeeeeeeeeeeeee of the cicadas. It was so simple, so obvious. Things were not going to become ok. They were already perfect.

I was reminded of my first orgasm at thirteen. Even though I had been aware of immense sexual frustration, knew intuitively that ejaculation would somehow let off the pressure, I had no idea that men had orgasms. All the magazines I encountered were full of articles about the "female orgasm," its myths and realities, but no one so much as suggested that men could come, too. My dad certainly never said anything.

So when an eighth grade friend shared his easily learned technique, I had no idea what lay in store. The abrupt sensation that the top of my skull had blown off, allowing a river of liquid sunlight to simultaneously pour in and pour out, took me so by surprise that I actually stopped moving my hand for a moment. Why had no one ever told me about this?

And as I sat within my vision circle, my whole body exploding in light, I realized no one had told me about this, either. And, unlike an orgasm, this feeling went on and on, both my head and my heart getting bigger and bigger, expanding way beyond my body, until my joy contained everything that existed. For hours, I just lay on the ground radiating bliss. No sexual experience, no drug, had prepared me for this. My vision question had not only been answered, but the answer was so much larger and more joyful than anything I could ever have hoped for. I hadn't just solved my personal riddle; I had cracked the code of existence. The answer was right there where everybody could see it, everybody could have a piece. And it had been there the whole time.

And, slowly, just as with all the sensations before it, this joy gradually, imperceptibly subsided, shrank down, vanished over the horizon. Just the same, I knew I had been shown something very important. I would never be the same.

But there was a sense of bafflement, bewilderment. What was that? How could I possibly communicate it to anyone else? A two letter word—Be— was never going to convey what had just happened. And, finally, would I ever get to taste something like that again?

What I didn't know, couldn't yet know, was that I had just been given a taste of the ultimate yogic goal, *Samadhi,* a flash of what Buddha experienced under the Bodhi tree: enlightenment. So interesting that the French slang for "orgasm," *petit mort,* or "little death," echoes the Sanskrit word for "death," *mahasamadhi,* or "big liberation." It's not just that sex and death are connected, but orgasm and spiritual liberation are as well.

But, I had no language for what had just happened. It wouldn't be for another thirteen years, when I finally met the guru and encountered the writings of Eckhart Tolle, that I was to learn the significance of what I had just experienced: *ananda,* the bliss of being, the joy that lies within and beneath all creation, accessible only to those who have stilled their minds, quieted their thoughts enough to become aware of its omnipresence.

With this ecstatic experience of Be! I was a like a kid who is hoping for a toy car and is given a Cadillac. But not only did I not know how to drive, I couldn't reach the pedals. I had gone into the woods to get some instructions about my next move and God had seen me and raised me, blasting me with a joy that I had not expected, even imagined.

The fourth and final day of my vision quest was spent in a daze as I attempted to comprehend what I had experienced, tried to find a way not to let go of it. Instead, slowly and inexorably, the usual mundane thoughts flooded back in and I returned to my life, my ruined marriage.

Chapter 5

You Can't Be a Hollow
Bone if You're Full of Shit

Not long after my quest, I got a twelve-step sponsor and started going to meetings every week. In large part, this was due to my father. He began his work in addiction research when I was a little boy and it had led him to AA, not as a member, but to recognize it as the single most effective solution to alcoholism. This was not a popular notion in his field of psychiatry, but his research clearly showed that the twelve-step approach was far more effective than traditional therapy.

He always spoke positively about AA, even taking me to a meeting when I was fifteen. He knew then that I was a "problem drinker." I remember listening in fascination to people tell the most awful stories about what had happened to them. "Thank God I wasn't like them," I thought. I didn't know that most fifteen-year-olds don't black out every time they drink.

So, in the spring of 1997, when a friend suggested that I might find a meeting helpful, I didn't argue. Filled with shame and remorse for how I had betrayed Nancy, I was desperate to make some kind of amends. However, this isn't how the program works. Amends aren't even mentioned until Step Eight. Until I had at least a passing notion of concepts like humility, gratitude, compassion, any "amends" I tried to make would be hollow.

I felt at home in the meetings immediately. The air was thicker in the room, like the atmosphere of your favorite bar. But here it wasn't cigarette smoke and the smell of beer that made the air palpable. Entering the room for my first meeting, I'd felt goose bumps, that involuntary shiver I'd begun to recognize as my built in "Geiger counter" for the presence of spirit.

It wasn't just the vibrations in the air. Things people said were challenging me to think differently, too. In my past, the word "humility" meant "humiliation," getting my face rubbed in shit. But now, I heard the word in a new way, as a counterpoint to the arrogance of an active alcoholic. I became increasingly aware of the entitlement running through my drinking, my drugging, my sleeping around. I did these things because I "deserved" to feel better, the hell with anybody else. I began to realize that the word, "high," meant putting myself above others. "Humility" didn't mean being degraded. It meant being sober.

Another word that began to jump out was "gratitude." When that word first came up at a meeting, I had to laugh. What did I have to be grateful for? I couldn't drink. I was in the doghouse with my wife and a lot of folks in my community saw me as an asshole. When it was my turn to share about what I was grateful for, I answered, "Nothing."

But as they say in the rooms, "Keep coming." Or, "Take the cotton out of your ears and put it in your mouth." My sponsor had told me to keep quiet for six months. I had a lot to learn and a bunch of this stuff wouldn't make sense for a while.

One of the things I didn't like about the twelve-step program was the absence of a guarantee. I wanted a promise that things were going to get better, that I was going to get better. I wanted a return on my investment, my sacrifice. I had given up drinking after all. But all I heard was a bunch of suggestions. So when I first heard the saying, "A grateful heart will never drink," I sat up and paid attention. This was a guarantee!

Gratitude wasn't just coming up in meetings. It is the cornerstone of all Native American spirituality. In this system, you had to thank everything. I was learning to make tobacco offerings to the four directions, special trees, rocks, streams... My son, Kirby, helped me with this. He was three now and we spent a lot of time watching The Muppets. We both loved the show and he insisted on watching the vhs tapes over and over until we could sing along with the huge muppet monsters (Kirby called them "monnies") doing Cole Porter— our favorite was "I've Got You Under My Skin."

Walking in the woods with Kirby one day, I noticed an especially captivating White Birch, its shining branches reaching out in all directions as if it were dancing. I was just reaching into my tobacco pouch to make an offering, when Kirby stopped and pointed at the tree. "Monny!" I was puzzled at first. Was he frightened? But then I realized he was making an association with the larger Muppets characters— their inarguable power. As this synchronicity repeated itself— me noticing a tree or stone with numinous energy and Kirby, a beat later, pointing and calling out "Monny!"— I realized he was my teacher. Learning to "see like a shaman" meant redeveloping a three-year-old's openness to the power of nature. Every time he called out, it was like getting a gold star; I was making a correct identification.

I felt self-conscious about my tobacco offerings at first. It felt ridiculous to be offering something, saying "Thank you," to a tree. But, after a while, just the physical act of offering—of reaching my hand into my tobacco pouch, formulating a silent prayer, extending a gift—began to shift something inside me. I felt a softening, a loosening. I didn't have to be clenched in resentment or anxiety all the time. I could surrender

66

into a much more delicious appreciation for what lay around me. It felt really good to say "Thank you."'

Just the same, the sheer number of infidelities shattered any possibility of trust between Nancy and me. I was reminded of the time we had gotten lost driving through Brooklyn, where we lived for nine years. It was like some kind of international tour as every few blocks we passed through a different ethnic region, streets filled with Jamaicans, stores festooned in green, black and gold, and then the lights changed and everyone was yelling in Chinese. As we passed through a miniature Dominican Republic, I saw, out of the corner of my eye, a large stuffed animal fall from a second story window. I turned my head and saw it was a boy. I watched as he crumpled on the ground and then instinctively got up, tried to walk. He didn't realize his legs were broken and I was horrified to see him crumple again. People began pouring out of the building, running towards him, and then the light changed. We were swept away.

Our marriage was that little boy. We had hit the ground, but the full extent of the damage was not immediately evident. As if in slow motion, we were trying to get up—going to couples counseling, having sex, trying to be kind to each other. We did not yet realize that the legs of our relationship were beyond repair. We would never walk together again.

I remember sitting in bed together, each of us reading, and noticing the books we held. She was intently studying *The Artist's Way* and I was reading *The Way of the Shaman.* We were on different paths now. We had met in a class on American Romanticism in college, taught English at the same private school in Brooklyn for six years, but now upstate, following our individual bliss, we were being taken in different directions. Artists and shamans are cousins, but the currents of joy that carried us were pulling us farther and farther apart. I wasn't much interested in her poetry and she felt my increasing tendency to seek guidance from my "imaginary" shamanic journeys was evidence of mental illness.

During this time, a year after my vision quest, I went to another shamanic workshop—"The Path of the Soul," taught by Christina Stack. I knew I would be in for a powerful weekend. I also knew my track record at these workshops—the incredible rush of spiritual energy I experienced could so easily slide into romantic infatuation with its attendant consequences. I vowed to Nancy and myself that I had learned my lesson and would stay on the straight and narrow. As I drove south to the Catskills, I kept repeating these vows. No more screw ups!

As soon as I was seated in the circle of workshop participants, I found myself scoping the room, picking out prospective women. I just couldn't help it. I worked hard to keep my eyes down.

There was one woman in particular that my eyes kept returning to. She had long, dark wavy hair, a small heart shaped face with a button nose, that kind of "fairy tale princess" look which always undid me. In fact, she was uncannily similar to a woman in a dream I had back at college, a dream that haunted me ever since:

I soar on huge wings over a triple-trunked oak. (I would learn later that, in Siberia, such trees are associated with great shamanic power.) There is a platform between the trunks on which are standing three women— an old grandmother, a middle-aged woman, and a beautiful young woman with long wavy dark hair who looks like a princess. I am captivated by her and realize I am flying for her, showing her what kind of man I am.

But I want her to know that I am not just about display, that I have serious attributes. Beside the tree is a lake and in the lake, I believe, might be monsters. I will rid the lake of them. Diving down into the water, I swim to the bottom, but there are only reeds and sand. Swimming to the surface, I realize that I have not fully thought through my actions. I might be suave and graceful in the air, but in the water my wings are soaked, heavy, dragging me down. I flail, start to drown. And then, just in time, the young princess reaches down from the platform and pulls me to safety.

I had awoken from that dream filled with longing and for years had kept my eye out for that woman. She had never showed up. But now I couldn't take my eyes off her. Even more concerning was that I kept seeing her as pregnant, which she wasn't. And I was the father. Even though there had been countless women over the years whom I'd imagined myself sleeping with, not once had pregnancy resulted and never once had I imagined myself as the father of their children. What kind of fantasy would that be? Every time I looked across the room, I saw her belly swelling and I knew it was our child, a daughter.

As it turned out, my room was directly over hers. In fact, my bed was directly above her bed. I was already lying on top of her. And, that first night, every time I closed my eyes and allowed myself to think of her, we were going at it— our bodies entangled, moving together, breath coming in pants. It took every ounce of willpower to think about something else.

In the morning, I awoke early, unable to sleep. To take my mind off who lay beneath me, I went out into the woods for a walk. Nothing like a little exercise to clear the mind. As I worked to keep my mind off this woman, a phrase surfaced in my thoughts:

You can't be a hollow bone if you're full of shit.

I loved it! What a great play on the shamanic expression, "hollow bone," one who allows spirit to flow through without obstruction. I might be telling myself I was happily married, now faithful to my wife, but it was crap.

At lunch, I pulled up a chair next to this woman. I had to see her face up close. Was she the woman from my dream? She introduced herself as Tracey. She was easy to talk to and told me she lived in Kentucky. I had lived in Kentucky. We had something in common.

As the workshop went on, I kept finding myself sitting with her. We were each diving into shamanism with both feet. She was already in

Michael's three-year program which met two weeks a tear for three years. I wondered if I could get in, too.

During the final journey of the weekend, we were instructed to ask our guides what the first thing was that we should do to start following our soul's path. I journeyed to Bear, who told me I should offer Tracey a Reiki treatment. I figured it must be a test. Would I be able to lay my hands all over Tracey's body and remain devoted to my wife? Kind of like Odysseus and the Sirens.

After the workshop, I screwed up my courage and asked Tracey if I could give her a Reiki treatment. She seemed pleasantly surprised and we went to her room. After I finished, I congratulated myself for making it through without it becoming something else. Now I could go home. I'd passed the test.

"That was so nice of you," she said. "Let me do a healing for you."

I said that wasn't necessary, but she insisted.

I sat on the edge of the bed and she knelt behind me. She put her arms around me, laying them over my heart. I closed my eyes as she softly sang. She had the sweetest voice. A glow filled my chest. It was like she was filling me with honey. I felt golden, so happy, so filled with peace. I had been looking for this feeling my entire life.

We said our goodbyes. I would never see her again. At home, I tried to push Tracey out of my mind as my wife wept beside me. Her cat's kittens were slowly dying, one each night, and there was nothing she could do.

At work two days later, helping a friend build a cabin, I still couldn't shake the feeling. That glowing in my chest as Tracey reached her arms around me, as if I were being slowly filled with warm golden light. It wasn't sexual. Just the same, it was a feeling I wanted more than anything else I had ever felt. Jim Morrison's words reverberated in my head: "No eternal reward will forgive us now for wasting the dawn."

Action was needed. If I waited, I would never see this woman again. Mumbling some kind of excuse to my friend, I was behind the wheel of my truck, making the two-hour drive south.

"What are you doing here?" Tracey stopped midstride through the retreat center cafeteria as I appeared in front of her. We walked through the woods as I poured out my heart. I shared my predicament, my broken marriage. I wasn't asking her to have an affair. I wanted to marry her. There were just some details I had to take care of.

"Why don't you come here and kiss me." We were sitting on a bench now and Tracey was trying to get a word in. I really didn't want to. I felt I needed to sort my life out first. But Tracey told me later she had to know how I kissed before she let things go any further.

I had planned to wait to tell Nancy when we were at our weekly couple's counseling session. I did not look forward to weathering her reaction by myself. But she could feel my energy shift, knew I was gone, before we got to the appointment. "You have to go, " Nancy announced one morning as we had coffee in bed. "You just aren't here anymore."

And that was it. My first marriage was over. I moved out. Got a lawyer. Started making plans with Tracey for my new life. Nancy and I were done. I felt huge relief. Leaving my four-year-old son was another thing. That broke my heart.

Before the recent workshop, I had arranged for him to ride in the cab of a locomotive, blow the horn. Trains were a shared passion and we spent hours "train chasing," riding the country roads in search of big freights and following them for as long as we could. Sometimes we'd wind up in Albany or even Schenectady, over fifty miles away. I had a friend who was an engineer on a small local rail line and he agreed to let us ride one day. As Kirby pulled the rope to sound the air horn, he shouted, "This is the best day of my life!" Now, three weeks later, I was treating him to the worst day.

Just the same, the inner voice was clear. "You have to do this. Your life depends on it." And I had no doubt this was true. Nancy and I were making each other miserable. Members of my family confided in me after I moved out how relieved they were. It wasn't that they approved of my getting a divorce. "It's just the tension in the house, the tension between you and Nancy, was unbearable."

I moved to an apartment in town, saw Kirby on the weekends. During that first winter apart, Nancy was understandably furious. "What a waste!" she said to me in the driveway, hands on her hips. Maybe. But there was no way we could have stayed together. She believed where I was going was diagnosable. I felt she was stuck. Under these words lay the wreckage.

Chapter 6

Spirit Hollow

Tracey and I knew from the start that we wanted to run a shamanic center and started looking for land as soon as she moved up from Kentucky. She found a job teaching English at a small local college while I spent my free time going to realtors. We didn't have much of a budget, but Nancy and I sold our house—we each wanted a fresh start—which gave me something to work with.

Just down the road from the old house was a large wilderness area— 5000 acres of National Forest surrounded by 25,000 acres of privately held lumber land, terrain for the most part too steep and inaccessible ever to be developed. This is where I did my first vision quest. A dirt road led to the center of this area and then stopped, unable to go further. Somewhere in there would be perfect. So when one realtor told me about a parcel near the end of that dirt road, I was intrigued. However, it was almost two hundred acres, far more than we could afford. "Check it out," the realtor replied. "I guarantee you will like what you see."

Two hours later, standing on a ridgeline, trees as far as I could see, clear silence ringing in my ears, I realized I had been here before. Nine months earlier— April 1998, two years after my first vision quest— in preparation for my second vision quest in Utah, I had done a "medicine walk" in this same wilderness area. A solitary walk in nature while fasting from food and water, the medicine walk prepares the supplicant for his time of sacrifice, from the Latin word meaning "to make sacred." Starting from the ring of logs where I had done my first quest, I had set out for the summit of the mountain. It hadn't been hard to find. Just keep going up until you can't. Coming down, however, is another thing entirely.

I had told no one before setting off. I figured I would be only gone a couple of hours. I had not brought any food or water, certainly not a map or compass or flashlight. What kind of "medicine walk" would that be? Tracey was still in Kentucky. As I looked out from the summit, I realized I hadn't done a very good job of noting landmarks for my return. Still, I had a rough sense of the direction I had come up from and headed that way.

It didn't take long before I was lost. The slope I was going down was much steeper than the one I'd come up and I was descending into a dense forest. Surely by now I should be seeing some kind of habitation in the distance? The sun was setting. It was early April and, at this altitude, there were still several inches of snow on the ground. Soon it would be dark and cold and I would be in real trouble.

I stopped and inhaled deeply. Panic wasn't going to help. Taking a slow 360 degree assessment, I realized that I was heading in the wrong direction. That perilously steep slope I had been descending for the last half an hour? I was going to have to climb it if I wanted to get home. I was hungry, thirsty and lightheaded. My legs had zero interest in going up, but I had no choice.

There was a stream running beside me, filled with snowmelt, the only sound in these woods. If I didn't break my medicine walk fast and drink, there was no way I would be able to climb back up the steep slope. I knelt and drank deeply, the icy water burning my throat. I was able to climb to the ridge, get my bearings, and descend to my car just as the last light left the sky.

Now, standing on this ridge nine months later, I could see the ravine I had descended that April day. It led right to the end of the road I was parked along now.

Back on the road, I saw a handwritten sign advertising a much smaller parcel, something we could afford. A couple of days later, Tracey and I were walking the parcel, discussing potential building sites, though we weren't crazy about being so close to a road. It was February now and after a couple of hours we were ready to head home and have some soup. As we got back to my locked truck, I reached in my pocket for my keys. They weren't there.

Tracey looked at me with a mixture of pity and irritation. I was reminded of the old joke about why it takes three hundred million sperm to fertilize one egg. Because none of them will ask for directions. I was in a worse predicament. I wasn't going to have to ask a stranger for directions. I was going to have to ask him for a ride home.

As it turned out, the nearest house was owned by the crankiest man in the hollow, the last guy you would ever want to ask for a favor. And he sure wasn't going to help me out that day. Instead, he dispatched his daughter to drive us home. On the ride, she regaled us with all the gossip along the road. Who had divorced whom, who was about to get foreclosed on. She mentioned an old man who lived at the very end of the road, at the very heart of this wilderness.

"That's Joe Murray. Crazy old guy. Sometimes he takes a walk past our house, always has two six shooters in holsters. To tell you the truth, he gives me the creeps. Kind of like that guy in *The Texas Chainsaw Massacre*. I heard he sold a bunch of land to the National Forest last year, but I think he still has a hundred acres the family is trying to sell. They don't want him living out there by himself anymore."

As soon as I got home, I looked Joe Murray up in the phone book. He answered on the second ring. I asked him if he had some land for sale. "Yup."

Two days later, Tracey and I were standing at the end of Shaftsbury Hollow Road looking up a stream bed. That was all that was left of the long driveway coming down from Joe's house. We knew that the parcel he owned, one hundred acres with a year-round stream running through it, was completely surrounded by National Forest which, in turn, was surrounded by an even larger area of wild land. The biggest Vermont wilderness area outside the Green Mountains. I also knew something else. This brook, which ran through this land like a central artery, was the same stream I had broken my vow to drink from nine months before. I felt like Persephone when she finally succumbed to Hades' temptations and ate a handful of pomegranate seeds; now I was required to return to what had looked to me at the time like a very dark and cold and scary place. The kind of place where you could die.

Tracey and I walked up the driveway. What would we find around that bend several hundred yards ahead? What we saw was a derelict shack surrounded by every kind of junk you could think of—old cars, lawn mowers, refrigerators, bedsprings. As we got closer, there was a smell, too. Burning plastic and rancid meat.

Joe was out front. "Sorry I didn't get a chance to clean up," he said without a trace of irony. As I shook hands with him, I realized he wasn't looking at me. He was staring at Tracey's chest. Tracey had to bend down to get his attention, break the spell.

Joe began his sales pitch. This was the family homestead, built by his father from discarded poles he had picked up when he worked for the power company. The man had enlisted his sons in the building effort, which stretched over several years. When it was completed, dad moved the family out to live there permanently and the project began.

Imagine living in the same place for fifty years and never taking your trash away. Every vehicle, every appliance, every egg carton you ever used, stays. Imagine the amount of miscellaneous debris arranged around your home, with the greatest concentration around the back door. Nothing goes any farther than you can carry or throw it. It's not an easy look to achieve. But here it was. And it could be ours for the right price.

Joe lived with his parents after he left school and stayed on after both of them passed. We learned later that local rumor suggested that the father and son simply "stepped over the body" for two weeks after the mother died. We weren't sure she had ever left. The house was permeated not only by the smell of multiple species' urine (human, cat, rodent), but there was an overwhelming odor of putrefaction.

As he took us through the house, Joe apologized again for not having cleaned up. The only thing that could have cleaned this place up was the Army Corps of Engineers. The stink and filth was knee deep. Multiple TVs littered the living room. The bathroom consisted of a toilet set over an open hole in the floor above a dirt cellar. There was no actual plumbing. The kitchen featured a large dead rat stretched across the floor (this was during a warm May) and the inside of the refrigerator looked like it had recently hosted a months' long food fight among tiny people, the once white interior splattered from top to bottom with layers of myriad foodstuffs. It contained no actual food.

"I guarantee you will like what you see," the realtor had said about the other parcel. Here it wasn't what we saw, but what we imagined that stole our hearts. This location on a hundred wooded acres, with a stream running through it, surrounded by thousands of acres of National Forest land was something you could look for during a couple of lifetimes and still not find. We had been guided to this place. On a site like this, you could do whatever you wanted and never bother anybody with your weird goings on. It's hard to do a sweat lodge—big fire, songs and drums, naked people—in the 'burbs.

We soon learned that we would not be negotiating with Joe, but with his brothers who had gotten out of that place as soon as they could. They were concerned about the conditions their brother was sinking into and wanted him to move to a trailer in town. However, he was the point person, which suited us just fine. His interpersonal skills and approach to home décor seemed to have scared off any prospective buyers, leaving us as the only people interested in striking a deal.

Actually, other buyers hadn't had a chance. There was no realtor. Joe hadn't put an ad in the paper or even posted signs. The place was just, existentially, for sale. Apparently, the only way to learn of it was to lose your keys in the woods and ask for a ride from the talkative daughter of a very grouchy neighbor.

We settled on a price of $500 an acre, unheard of in Vermont in 1999. After the closing, Joe pleaded for an extra two weeks to move out. Realizing his adjustment to village life would be hard, we agreed. We felt a little bad about driving him out. Left up to him and his sales campaign, he figured he would never have to leave. However, when we returned two weeks later, in mid June, we found the house abandoned, locked up tight. The heavy metal front door was too hard to break down. I went around to the back and smashed the lock with a sledgehammer. I tried to push the door open, but it wouldn't budge.

As I struggled to get in, I became aware of a terrible smell, that putrefaction again. Looking around, I noticed an old washing machine sitting beside me on the back porch. It was a wringer washer from the fifties—a big open top agitator and, extending off the side, a hand operated wringer, two rollers side by side which you turned with a crank. The kind of contraption you would hate to get your hand caught in. As my eyes focused, I realized the agitator was filled to the brim with feces. This apparently was where Joe did his business when he got tired of shitting into the basement. Kicking it off the porch, I went back to shoving against the door, but it was stuck on something. As I pushed and heaved, a long thin object began to emerge from under the door: the tail of the dead rat I had observed two weeks earlier.

Finally inside, I could observe no change. Nothing appeared to have been removed from the house. Not the clothes all over the floor, the TVs, or the month's worth of dishes in the sink. The place was as cluttered with junk as it had been the day we bought it. And then I saw her.

Standing sadly, hands in prayer, a garland of roses around her neck, was a three-foot statue of St Theresa of the Little Flowers. I had no idea who she was at that moment, but this was no place for a lady. I picked her up as if I were rescuing her and took her down to the stream and washed her in the water. She would never have to go back into that house. In fact, a few nights later, the volunteer fire department came and burned the place to the ground.

About twenty of our friends came to the "house warming," and there were about twenty volunteer firemen as well. It turned out there were three structures to get rid of: the original house, a trailer home, and a collapsing barn. Joe had thoughtfully left us about a hundred gallons of fuel oil in a tank so we had plenty of fire starter.

The firemen were especially excited. "We don't often get called to burn folks' houses down, ma'am," one of them confided in Tracey. They got the three buildings going in the late afternoon and used the smoking house for a training exercise. We watched as they cut a hole in the roof to release smoke and took turns viewing the house through an infrared camera and entering it with oxygen masks.

By eight in the evening, all three buildings were really going. I stood at the center point among three infernos, feeling as if my head was about to explode. My whole body was trembling. The adrenaline pouring through me was, a friend told me later, enough to kill a housecat. All my life, people had been telling me I was "too much": too loud, too hyper, too crazy, too intense. As a teenager, I loved burning things—model airplanes, sticks and leaves, anything I could put a match to. I was called "Pyro" and it made me feel ashamed.

But here I was in the middle of more fire than I had ever seen. And not only that, but I had struck the match. And the most amazing thing was that I wasn't in trouble. Everybody was smiling and laughing, friends and firemen alike.

As I stood surrounded by three fully engaged structure fires, flames licked the air as high as the trees, roaring and crackling, completely out of control. The heat was almost too much to take, but the message was clear: Set the world on fire with joy and only good will come from it.

And then came fifteen months of the hardest work I had ever done: clearing the land for the geodesic dome we planned to live in. Whereas "clearing land" in Vermont usually means cutting down trees, grading a site, building an access road; here it meant getting rid of the forty tons of crap that remained after we burned everything down. We filled dumpster after dumpster with endless ceramic and metal, booty from fifty years of never going to the dump, never letting anything go.

Along the way, we built a yurt that we lived in while building our house. We'd later use it as a space for teaching shamanic workshops. We might have only been shamanic practitioners for a couple of years, but all of those workshops with Michael Harner had given us a good idea of how to proceed.

We were on fire for shamanism. It had changed our lives and we knew first hand that it provided a powerful modality for changing the way you see the world. If people learned how to journey, they would live in a whole new way—seeing birds and animals and trees and rocks and mountains as "people," too. And not just ordinary people, but beings with ancient and powerful wisdom to guide and enlighten. We knew these shamanic techniques could save the world and we wanted to be part of that. Spirit Hollow, Tracey's name for our shamanic center, was born when we set up that first yurt. Our motto was "Transforming consciousness."

Over the next year, I learned why you see so few geodesic domes. Despite all the enthusiasm when Buckminster Fuller first loosed them on the world, they are very hard to build. The external shell goes up quickly. But putting a roof on it, hanging sheet rock, dividing it into usable living space? That was another thing.

And so, while the shell went up in a weekend, it took me and another man, using power tools, over five weeks to put on 3000 square feet of asphalt shingles, a job that should take a week on a normal house. And it was like that with everything. Hanging the sheet rock was like being trapped in a geometry exam for two months. During a very cold winter. There were few full triangles, mostly parts of them. An old friend with a long time in the building trades surveyed our progress when we were about halfway through and pronounced solemnly, his words turning to steam in the freezing air, "You guys are in sheetrock hell."

But, after a year, it came to an end. We had a house that looked like an igloo. Perfect for shamans. We cleared out the yurt and used it as a space to teach classes on how to journey. Our students came from all over New England and many experienced positive transformations in their lives—new jobs, new creative undertakings, new relationships. In our own small way, we felt we were making a difference.

My son, Kirby, was seven now and he was struggling. He had an androgynous nature— loved wearing dresses and make up— and recently started experimenting with nail polish. This didn't fly at Cambridge Central School. Although urban refugees like Nancy and me had been tipping the demographic, the area had long been to the right of Attila the Hun. People still sported bumper stickers about "Hanoi Jane," twenty years after Jane Fonda's trip to North Vietnam, and the local congressman had recently told Patrick Kennedy (Ted Kennedy's son) that he didn't care what had happened to his family; gun ownership was a God-given right.

Although Nancy and I had no problem with Kirby's choices (we were Oberlin graduates after all), we feared for his safety. Our decision to ban him from wearing anything to school that wasn't "gender appropriate" was met with wails of protest. It demoralized him; even though he resumed dressing normally, his school mates never let him forget his unconventional dress. In desperation, I journeyed to my spirit teacher for guidance. What could I do for my boy? My teacher told me to take a father-son trip to a place of Kirby's choosing.

When Kirby cheerfully selected Niagara Falls as his dream vacation, I groaned inwardly. Several days at "America's favorite holiday destination" sounded awful. However, we found a quiet campsite on the banks of Lake Ontario and had a wonderful time getting soaked at the "Cave of the Winds" and aboard Maid of the Mist. Together, we discovered Native legends about the Falls and trails along the river below. The Niagara Gorge is a deadly section of rapids which reach speeds of more than 20 mph and are some of the most extreme in the world. Hiking so close to its undulating power thrilled us. Along the gorge cliffs we found first growth White Cedar over eight hundred years old. Kirby had found a "keeper" and we were to return together every summer for the next several years. School didn't become easy for him, but he was making friends and finding his way.

Chapter 7

Meeting the Guru

As Tracey and I were creating Spirit Hollow, I finally enrolled in Michael Harner's three-year shamanic training program, which met for two weeks a year for three years. Michael and his assistant, Sandra Ingerman, openly discussed their fascination with "miracles," otherwise inexplicable events that fulfilled prayers or deep longings, and their intention to replicate the conditions necessary to produce them.

At the beginning of the second year of the program, Michael had a stroke. Although he would recover partially, I never saw him again. At that point, his protege, Sandra Ingerman, took over. She remained my spiritual teacher for the next ten years. Sandra had taken Michael's interest in miracles to the next level: exhaustively searching for verifiable miracles—extraordinary transformations which could not be scientifically explained and which had reliable witnesses—and closely examining the conditions which had led to these events.

After years of careful study, Sandra discovered seven conditions which were always present when the miraculous occurred: intention + union + love + focus + concentration + harmony +imagination. She also came up with a series of journeys which helped participants enter the state of faith and surrender necessary to creating these conditions. In order for us to sustain this altered state, Sandra would have us tone a sound that best expressed what we were feeling. Toning is a form of vocalizing that utilizes the natural voice to express sounds ranging from cries, grunts, and groans to open vowel sounds and humming on the full exhalation of the breath. Music therapists utilize toning in their clinical practice for a variety of therapeutic aims. Because she had always had a deep, heartfelt connection to the oceans, to water, Sandra focused her efforts on creating a ceremony to purify contaminated water.

At first, she and her students worked with gasoline-poisoned water, but the fumes were too toxic. After more research, she came upon another common contaminant that did not poison the air as well: sodium hydroxide. A common agricultural byproduct, this chemical makes it much easier for petroleum products to disperse in water (as opposed to simply pooling on the surface). This in turn enables them to more widely poison bodies of water and to travel much farther up the food chain.

During a workshop with her, I was introduced to the ceremony she had created for purifying water. She would intentionally poison a container of water with the sodium hydroxide, turning the water into a deadly brew, its toxicity confirmed by a pH test. At the end of the ceremony, perhaps thirty minutes later, another pH test was done. It declared the water to be potable. With me at the workshop were MDs and PhDs, present as Sandra's students and as trained skeptics. In the conversation that followed, I learned there was no scientific explanation for what had just happened. Through natural evaporation, the pH could have gone down a little, after two weeks. However, the water still would not have been safe to drink.

What blew me away about the ceremony wasn't the water purification itself. What stayed with me was how the ceremony made me feel. After the preliminary journeys, where we were guided to let go of our egoic personalities and merge with unconditional love, we all stood in a circle, toning to maintain our altered states. The room filled with an angelic chorus as our individual toning found its way into multilayered harmonies which rose and fell like ocean swells. Three people with serious illnesses lay at the center of the circle to receive these healing energies most directly. Some of us were guided to kneel by them and lay on hands. As I knelt at the center of the circle, laying my hands on a dear friend with no other intention than to send her unconditional love, toning all the while, I found myself held in undulating waves of sound pouring over me from all directions. Suspended in this sonic ocean, I felt weightless, warmed and comforted by a deep tenderness.

I was not prepared for the pure joy I felt in the company of so many people. Held in the stream of ninety chanting voices, I was blessed. I was healed. I was perfected. The vibrating air, a flood of the sweetest syrup, penetrated my bones. Love was pouring into me and, as I continued to tone, love was pouring out. I could feel it streaming out of my hands into my friend and also shining out of her. Gradually, of its own accord, the volume of our toning gradually subsided, until we were in silence.

Afterwards, sitting in the original circle, I spoke quietly with two friends. At first, we just stared at each other, dumbfounded. None of us had ever felt like so happy, so joy-filled, so at peace—at the same time, in the same way, with so many others. As we wondered quietly to each other if this is what it felt like to be with Jesus, another member of the circle, unable to contain herself, began dancing and singing, moving slowly around the room. As she came around to us, we could hear her words: "Ask and it shall be given. Knock and the door will be opened…" Sandra made her way around the room as well. Tears in my eyes, I thanked her for sharing this extraordinary knowledge. She smiled. "How could I keep it to myself?"

When I returned home and embraced her, Tracey's first words to me were, "You love me differently." She was staring at me, her hands on my shoulders. "You love me larger. I can feel it." And it was true. I did love her differently, but it wasn't just her. I loved differently. It was as if that feeling I had when we first met, when she first laid her hands on my heart—the feeling I had been looking for my entire life—was now in my heart on its own. This feeling was my own natural radiance.

At the next workshop with Sandra, she told a story about the Indian guru Sai Baba. That word, "guru," repelled me. I associated it with fraud, self-abasement and abuse. I had heard stories of so-called "gurus" and none of them ended well. However, Sandra presented the story as a case study, a description of events seen by credible witnesses that could not be otherwise explained. And because I knew a little about the miraculous feelings Sandra could evoke, I was paying attention.

She began by describing a friend of hers who had lost her wedding ring down a sink in her Florida home in the 1980's. Just last year, nineteen years after losing the ring, the friend made a trip to India and stayed for a couple of days at Sai Baba's ashram. While there, she had darshan (Sanskrit for "viewing") of the holy man himself. Sitting in a large room with two thousand other devotees, she watched the diminutive man appear on stage. He then descended and began to make his way through the crowd. It took hours as he moved slowly through the adoring throng. Finally, he was standing directly in front of Sandra's friend. Extending his hand, Sai Baba said in perfect English, "Have you been looking for this?"

In his hand was the wedding ring she had lost down her sink in Florida nineteen years before.

If anyone other than Sandra had been telling this story, I would have rolled my eyes. But in five years of working closely with her, I knew her to be a woman of immense integrity. She would not waste our time with fables.

Sandra continued. "Sai Baba was asked how he was able to perform such miracles and why ordinary people could not do such things. Sai

86

Baba smiled and replied, 'Oh, it is very simple: I know who I am and you do not.'"

This simple statement hit home. If I just knew who I REALLY was, I would have what I was looking for. Just as my six year-old self knew that the secret to ending boredom lay right before my eyes, the secret of life lay within this simple question.

Who am I?

I shared these stories with anyone I thought might be interested. Was it really that easy? Were we separated from authentic miracle workers by so thin a veil? This sounded doable.

Most people just smiled. But one man said it reminded him of a story medical intuitive and author, Carolyn Myss, told at one of her lectures. Although Sai Baba was known for manifesting precious objects, his most frequent miracle was to produce vibhuti, sacred ash, in his hand. In India, such ash is highly valued for its powers to bless and heal. Carolyn had been fortunate enough to obtain a pinch of Sai Baba's vibhuti on a trip to India and she kept it on a special place on her altar.

Carolyn described a client coming to her in terrible straits. The woman was in complete despair and all Carolyn could think to do was give this woman her sacred ash. The woman was deeply grateful and left in an improved state of mind. Now it was Carolyn's turn to feel despair. She had been blessed enough to receive something so sacred from perhaps the greatest living saint on the planet and she had given it away!

The next day, a package arrived in the mail. It had been sent, surface post, from India months before and was battered from its journey. Holding the bundle in her hands, she was struck by its weight, its density. It was wrapped in brown paper, barely held together with string and tape, and covered with stamps, but the return address was illegible

Opening it, she could see it was a large plastic bag holding several pounds of fine, gray ash. A label on the bag identified it as coming from Sai Baba's ashram.

Again, I eagerly shared these stories, but when I told them to my friend, Bonnie, she smiled. "I always wondered what I should do with that." Reaching into a drawer, she pulled out a small paper packet. As she handed it to me, I could see the image of Sai Baba on the paper and the words "Sacred Vibhuti from His Ashram."

Soon after, I embarked on my third vision quest. My question was a direct response to Sai Baba: Who am I? And a nod to my shamanic training: what is my medicine?

Just as I had done with my previous two quests, I resolved to go without food or water for four days and nights. My friend, Rod, would accompany me to the nearby mountaintop and promised to check on me. Because most of the mountains in Vermont are below four thousand feet, they are covered with trees. However, the spot I chose was struck by lightning twenty years before. The resulting fire cleared several acres near the summit and trees never grew back. I would be questing in a small sea of ferns with a lovely view of the Green Mountains undulating to the east.

On my first morning, I placed the bag of sacred ash from Sai Baba at the center of the fern meadow, an offering to the mountain, and sat down to await my vision. On my previous quests, I had managed the lack of water fairly easily. By remaining still, staying out of the sun, moving as little as possible, four days without water was bearable. This time was different. Although it was still early May, the skies were clear and bright and held little humidity. In a large clearing high on a mountain, there was no way to escape the sun. I felt serious thirst pangs after a day. After two days, I began to feel sick.

Fortunately, Tracey had more sense than I did, insisting I bring a quart of water. Even though it seemed needless at the time, I was deeply grateful for it at the start of my second night. But it wasn't nearly enough. The nearest stream was an hour hike below, far out of reach for my hunger and thirst-weakened body. If I went down to drink, I would never make it back.

Rod and I had agreed on a spot a hundred yards into the woods where we could leave messages for each other. It was close enough that I could walk there easily, but not so close that I would be able to see or hear him come and go. I left a note for Rod asking him to leave any water he might have brought. When I returned to the spot, he had left me a pint.

The whole flavor of this quest was different from the others. The messages I received from the trees, the rocks, the birds—thoughts, feelings swirling and coalescing in my increasingly altered mind—were not nearly as welcoming as before. There was a challenging tone to them now, a hint of menace.

The low point came on the third day. Desperate to get out of the sun, I left the clearing and huddled in the shade of a red maple's trunk. Here follows an excerpt from my journal:

I make the traditional prayer of the *hanbleceya*, crying, literally weeping, for a vision: "I am small. I am pitiful. I am puny and weak, thirsty and hungry. Please give me something with which to feed my people."

Silence rings in my ears. I hear what sounds like the leaves breathing, the rise and fall of wind. And something else. Rising softly at first, then louder, clearer, words in my mind, unfamiliar: "Why should I tell you anything? You are one of them." The message continues, very similar to what the spruce and the oak have said over the previous two days: "Your prayers are very beautiful, but what are you wearing? Cloth, leather, taken from the earth without permission, without gratitude. What about the food that has formed you? No different. Taken in violence without seeing the damage done."

89

I answer feebly, saying something about how I am upset by the ATVs, the men who ride them, tearing up the woods, leaving a trail of beer cans, that I want to do something about them.

"ATVs?" the red maple snarls, "ATV's are nothing, pesky gnats. How about when the skidders come? Men with chain saws?"

I say I am bothered by that, too.

"Bothered? Bothered! Bothered by something that kills your entire family? Leaves your homeland a torn and muddy ruin, a wasteland! Bothered?!"

I say, "But the trees grow back. Look at this place now."

"You don't get it do you? You don't see that we are alive, too."

"But you don't feel pain the same way, do you?"

"That's what your kind always say about people they want to rape and murder and steal from. It's what they said about Africans and the people of this continent. It's what they say about anyone they oppress.

"Don't you see that we are no different than you? We retreat in winter and leap forth joyfully in spring. We propagate and create new life. We mate. We choose to live in the company of our relatives, our kind, in peace. Just because we cannot speak your language, or run, or fight, does not mean we do not feel our lives. We bleed, we heal our own wounds. Does that not show you we feel pain?

"Imagine, for a moment, that you are in your home with your family. Strange beings come to your house with huge, loud machines, screaming saws. They break down the walls of your house. They grab your son and cut him into pieces and throw him on a truck. They do the same to your wife, your parents, your brothers and sisters, your friends. And they do not even look at you or see that you are alive.

"Then they come for you. Or, worse, maybe only cut a piece off you and leave you. Or, worse still, don't even touch you, just leave you to live alone amidst the blood and ruin of their greed"

90

At this point, I burst into tears.

But the tree is not finished. "And it is not just once upon this mountain, but again and again. Even if you are able to rebuild your home, mate again, begin a new family, you know it is only a matter of time before they return.

"And it is not just on this mountain, but on every mountain in the world. And it is not just us Standing Ones who suffer, but all the four-leggeds. And not just the four-leggeds, but all the plant people. And not just the plant people, but the stone people. Look at how your kind cannot stop themselves from digging into the world everywhere you go and tearing at it and taking from it.

"And your people are still not satisfied, but they do the same to their own kind, like cannibals.

"What kind of vision can I give a people like you?"

I am sobbing now. "What can I do? What can I do?"

A small brown hawk glides low, two or three feet above the ferns, maybe twenty feet in front of me.

"You must look at what is in your people that makes them act this way and you must heal this sickness."

I did not realize it at the time, but I was having my first bare knuckled encounter with the Guru, a word which literally means "dispeller of darkness." At first, when we meet the Guru, we fall in love. Our hearts lift, our world expands. Everything is so beautiful. My early feelings about shamanism, my experience of "Beeee" on my first vision quest, are textbook examples of this. It was not a coincidence that, on that first quest, my mind had gone straight to Be Here Now, a book that was directly channeled by Ram Dass from his guru.   But later, once we are

91

good and hooked, things get real. The work begins. The dismantling of the ego. Death in slow motion.

The horror of what I had just experienced— being shown what I really was— completely bulldozed me. I had no idea what to do. The magnitude of my assignment overwhelmed me. Way beyond what the heroes in my favorite childhood stories had ever been told to do. I kept seeing myself spattered with the blood of everything I consumed. The truth of my life made me sick.

The first clue of what to do came two weeks later, at the final session of my three-year shamanic training. One of the tasks we were given was to create costumes and masks of our power animals and the "guides" or Spirit teachers who appeared in human form when we journeyed.

Our final "exam" was to stand up before our classmates in costume and mask and share a final word of guidance or offer healing. Watching people appearing as otherworldly beings was transfixing. Over the three years, we had all seen each other grow and change as we listened more and more carefully to our guides and to be able to finally meet them, see them, hear them, was very powerful. It is not often that we can so experience in physical form the interior world of another, see and feel their relationship with the divine.

As I watched and listened to a parade of bears and birds, saints and mythic beings, dance, sing, speak, I was deeply inspired. Each one shone with peace and wisdom and great kindness. But I was shaken by what I had experienced on the mountain. None of these positive messages touched the darkness I had been shown.

My bear found a way. As my turn came, and I lumbered around the circle wearing the skin of a grizzly that had been in my family for over a century, wearing a heavy wooden mask, carved from a long dead maple, I was drawn inexplicably to two of my classmates, or to their instruments. One woman had a leather rattle that fascinated me and I pawed at it as I went by. Another was holding a huge frame drum, which I smacked as I passed. Standing in front of the circle, my mind was blank, and then words erupted in a growling roar which made people jump. "The world is burning!" Bear growled. "What will you do?" I could see the planet in flames, feel a desperate sense of urgency. It was summer, 2001.

The next morning, I went over the event in my mind. I realized that something connected the two people whose instruments my "Bear" had been drawn to. The first woman was a devotee of Sai Baba. The other had recently gone to Brazil to receive healing from John of God. This healer worked with a group of invisible healers and had produced countless well-documented miracles. Although Sandra had also been to visit this healer and spoke of him often, no one else in the group spoke much of gurus. Our focus was on shamanism—what we had encountered in journeys or, for a few, Native American teachers.

What Sai Baba and John of God—the two "gurus" I was familiar with at that time— had in common was what I can only describe as the white light of Love, an unconditional and universal energy with unlimited transformational powers. The energy I had experienced in Sandra's transmutation ceremony.

What Bear seemed to be telling me—answering his question before he asked it— was that the only way to be of real assistance in this burning world was to get connected to this transforming Light. But how was I going to do that? Sandra's ceremony was transformative, but how could that energy be harnessed to help the whole world? I did not yet realize that Sai Baba was already guiding me in this very direction. It was no coincidence that his stories had gripped me so strongly, that his vibhuti had accompanied me to the mountaintop on my recent vision quest that had so powerfully shaken me. I was already being shown the way. I just didn't know it yet.

I returned from the final shamanic training session to the birth of my daughter, Maia, who arrived a few weeks later. It was a hard birth. Maia first presented face up, putting Tracey into back labor. Although this situation corrected itself, in all her twisting and turning, our daughter managed to wrap the umbilical cord around her neck and approached her mother's cervix in "military presentation," shoulders up and out as if standing at attention, basically making herself as big as possible as she approached this impossibly small opening. Odds were she would only come out through a Caesarian section, but Tracey was in the birthing tub at the hospital now, so close. We prayed—Tracey, the midwife and I– for our Maia to unclench, to surrender into birth. I knelt by the tub, holding Tracey's hand, and wept.

Minutes later, our daughter emerged into the world. Because there was meconium in the amniotic fluid due to the stress, her lungs had to be suctioned out before I could hold her, but her arrival in my arms was unforgettable. I can still feel her weight—solid, dense, inarguable- as I took her from the doctor. In our first embrace, I noticed that blood and shit were smeared on the walls.

It didn't get much easier. Because Tracey and I had "incompatible blood"—our blood types had opposing rH factors— Tracey's Rh factor was negative and Maia's was positive. Tracey's immune system made Rh antibodies that attacked her daughter's "foreign" red blood cells. The result was infant jaundice where the baby's blood contains an excess of bilirubin, a yellow pigment which results from destroyed red blood cells. It can be fatal and requires constant light therapy which breaks down bilirubin into a form that the body can get rid of through urine and stool.

Maia's first days of life were spent under bright lights, interrupted by trips back and forth to the hospital for repeated needle pricks in her feet for blood tests. Although our daughter emerged in fine health, her entry was traumatic and put all of us on edge. She slept with us in a big bed and nursed at will, but she awakened often in the middle of the night, screaming. She would be clean, dry, fed and burped, but remained inconsolable. Our doctor couldn't find anything wrong so the solution would be for me to walk with her, sometimes for hours in the darkness, singing softly, until she finally screamed herself to sleep.

She had more or less adjusted to life on earth by the time she turned one. My most vivid memory of Maia in her second year was watching her cuddle up with our big Golden Retriever, Bodhi, having festooned him with dolls' clothes. She would be naked and sprawled like a tiny odalisque on this enormous and infinitely patient ottoman of a dog. He was rewarded for his forbearance when he lay beneath her high chair as Maia dropped food from above. They had reached an understanding.

Chapter 8

Maharaj-ji

2003 was a big year for me. I turned forty-four that year and that was the age my grandfather was when he shot himself in the mouth on Mother's Day. I had always wondered why we never celebrated that holiday in our family, until I learned the date of his death. My dad was ten. He was the last person my grandfather had spoken to. "Have you seen the screwdriver," he asked my dad. Later, after, my father asked his mother, Sue, "Do you think he needed the screwdriver to fix his gun?"

I don't know if you ever get over suicide. Once that door has been opened in a family, it stays that way. So the depression that stalked me from thirteen, that sometimes settled right down to live with me for months at a time, would always have an added feature in its portfolio. Maybe it wasn't just a first name and high school alma mater that my grandfather and I would share.

I can still remember when my father first told me about it. I was six, standing in the room where I had the epiphany that everything I needed to be forever content lay right around me. "I want you to hear this from me, not through gossip," my father told me. "And you are not to speak of it to anyone." And, just like that, I knew what it really meant to be "George." Even though I was called by my middle name, Emery, everybody knew I was a George, too, fifth in a line of eldest sons—all named George.

So when I turned forty-four, my attention was focused. I had made it this far. The gun barrel had been in my mouth, too, a .30-30 Winchester, but the gun lock had been on the trigger and I had no idea where the key was. I never forgot the clink of metal against my teeth though, the taste of oil.

My grandfather had done it a month after his forty-fourth birthday. His wife, Sue, found him in the pouring rain, splayed out on the grass, the .45 Colt revolver still in his mouth. Spread all around his body were letters from his mistress, red spatters on the white stationary, smeared by the rain. The detective told Sue, "You know, the fingerprints were washed off the gun. For all we know, you could have shot him."

She fled the state after that. The shame. She took her kids and hid out for six weeks on her father's ranch in Arizona. My father remembers that time for the worst pain he ever experienced. One morning he put his foot into his boot without looking and learned, suddenly, that a scorpion had gotten there before him.

I could still feel the reverberations from that single shot all these years later. What was waiting for me in my forty-fifth year?

It was a very good birthday. I got some great gifts. My friend and neighbor, Felipe, gave me a life-sized Huichol jaguar head, the rainbow-colored beadwork shimmering in the sun. He and I shared a deep shamanic connection— a love for sweat lodge and working with the plant teachers in a sacred way. He was thanking me for my companionship. Another dear friend gave me an incredible hand-tooled leather "Shaman's belt," complete with bear designs, pouches for amulets, and a bone handled knife. Bruce made the belt himself and, while I only saw him every year or two (he lived in Ohio), this gift reminded me how close he really was.   The most amazing present I received that year, however, was a VHS cassette of a recently released documentary, *Ram Dass: Fierce Grace*.

Bill, the man who gave it to me, was godfather to Maia and Noah. Although his day job was performing oral surgery, he was a spiritual adventurer.   He and his wife had made several trips to the Amazon to participate in ayhuasca ceremonies and he was a practicing shaman, a committed meditator.   He was an elder brother for me, a door opener.

I knew of Ram Dass through his book, *Be Here Now*, the paradigm-shifting spiritual manual he co-wrote in the early seventies.   In his introduction, he briefly describes his transformation from privileged son of a wealthy tycoon to spiritual leader.   And this is where *Ram Dass: Fierce Grace* a begins.   The story it told was fascinating—how this young man from Boston, whose father was also a wealthy and famous George, had made it to Harvard as a professor of psychology, not unlike my own dad, and had then met Timothy Leary.   Run out of Harvard in disgrace after it came out that he and Leary had been "experimenting" on students, i.e., tripping with them, he finally found his way to India in despair.   Not because of losing his job, but because of frustration at touching enlightenment every time he took LSD and then returning to his old self every time he came down.   Maybe there was someone in India who could help him.

As it turned out, there was—Neem Karoli Baba, also known as Maharaj-ji, "great king," a common term of affection between men in India.   Ram Dass told of how, travelling in the Himalayan foothills, he had gone out to urinate one night and looked up at the stars.   They seemed especially bright and near and he found himself thinking of his mother, who had died a few months before of an enlarged spleen.   They had been very close.   The next day, he travelled with his friend to see the friend's guru, a word Ram Dass felt deep antipathy for, as I had.   Gurus were hucksters and charlatans, demanding undeserved adoration from their devotees.

98

This feeling was not lessened when he saw his friend lie down on his belly in the dust at the guru's feet, hands touching the man's toes. This was exactly what was wrong with gurus. After he had been introduced to Neem Karoli Baba, Ram Dass was struck by how familiar he was. "You were out under the stars last night," the old man said through an interpreter. "Good guess," Ram Dass thought, "Half of India was probably out under the stars last night." The man continued. "You were thinking of your mother. She died of, of," the guru paused, and then spoke in English, "Spleen."

And that was all it took. Ram Dass— then Richard Alpert—felt a painful cracking in the center of his chest. As his mind struggled and failed to find purchase, he started to sob. His heart had been opened. Richard Alpert's old life ended, and Ram Dass was born. *Be Here Now* was created soon after.

When Ram Dass had his stroke in 1997, he almost died and the after-effects were life altering. He could barely walk and his ability to speak— his greatest gift, source of prestige, and meal ticket—was severely impaired. He could still converse, but only with agonizing pauses. The immediate consensus of everyone, including him, was "poor Ram Dass."

However, after pursuing many healing avenues, including trips to John of God in Brazil, he came to realize that the grace of his guru, Neem Karoli Baba, Maharaj-ji, which had first enveloped him in 1967, had never, could never, leave him. And, if everything which had happened since that fateful day in the Himalayan foothills had been grace, then the stroke must be grace, too.

And this was the central message of the movie—how this tragic event was actually a ferocious form of grace. And seeing Ram Dass's later-in-life transformation into an even more peaceful and humble and grateful person, I could feel the truth of this revelation. Watching him speak, sit in silence, smile, I could feel how much more humble and at peace he was, compared to footage of him from shortly before the stroke, only four years earlier.

My first impressions of the documentary were twofold—felt and cognitive. The felt experience was a warm glowing feeling in my chest that I first associated with Ram Dass. The other was the concept of fierce grace. Grace I knew a little about, but the idea that it could be ferocious, traumatic, was a paradigm shift.

I recalled my own early childhood trauma, the abuse I had experienced when my mom was overcome by episodes of post traumatic stress disorder from her own terrible abuse as a child. She never drank like her own alcoholic mother, but she could go into violent and terrifying rages as if she had been drinking. This rage had deep roots. Her mother, Barbara, went into a deep depression when my mom was three and her sister was one. They were on Martha's Vineyard, West Chop, a summer community created in the 1880's by Barbara's grandfather and some business associates from Boston. Barbara was staying with her daughters in the immense shingled ark built by her parents, a mansion overlooking the ocean. When she thought her mother was out, Barbara mixed poison into a pot of tea and served herself and her daughters. She and my mom were on the living room floor when Barbara's mother returned unexpectedly. The doctor was called. Stomachs were pumped. No one died. But that was the moment my mom lost her mother, who was whisked off to Macleans Psychiatric Hospital and only allowed custody of her daughters for brief periods after that.

My mom's dad became her primary caregiver but he didn't have much more in the way of emotional resources. He'd lost his father when he was a boy. The loss, the resulting financial challenges, left him permanently needy. He had seen his lovely young wife as a move into prosperity and when that blew up, he leaned heavily on my mom, who was only three. Although my mother insists he did not abuse her sexually, he romanced her, giving my mom a "wedding" ring and cuddling her frequently. He quickly remarried, however, and no longer needed my mother. When she ran to him in tears, he hauled off and knocked her across the room. "Keep it to yourself," he hissed.

100

This ancient pain could explode out of my mother without warning whenever she felt overwhelmed by any of her children's needs. I only remember a few of these episodes, but many more were stored in my body. My depression, when I really came to understand it, was actually impacted terror, the feeling that I was about to die violently.

But what if, instead of abuse, my mother's behavior had been an extreme form of grace? What if her actions, as frightening as they might have been at the time, had actually been something else? What if my childhood trauma had actually been my soul on God's anvil? Just as the obscenity of the crucifixion becomes the radiant promise of Easter, just as Ram Dass's debilitating stroke became his guru's grace, what if my suffering were also in the service of some higher purpose?

I could not answer this question, but it had its teeth in me. A door had appeared, a possibility raised. There might be something to be grateful for in the wreckage of my childhood. Somewhere in those ruins, I knew now, lay the key to a completely different understanding of my life.

I was coming to learn that this key was gratitude, a word not in my vocabulary when I first got sober. But I had learned a lot about gratitude through the twelve steps. I had also learned a lot about "grace," another word I knew nothing of when I was drinking.

I began to associate these two words—gratitude and grace— with one another. They both come from the same Latin root, gratus, "pleasing, thankful," and vibrate at a similar frequency. A feeling of gratitude is a flash of grace: a weight lifted, a blessing bestowed. I worked to "cultivate an attitude of gratitude" (an expression I loathed in my drinking days.

Gratitude opens our awareness of a much larger and more beautiful world, a world pervaded by beauty and kindness, a world pervaded by grace. The concept of "fierce grace", a grace which initially appeared painful or terrifying, was an expansion of my understanding. If Ram Dass could feel grateful for having a stroke, anything was possible.

A few months later, I was sharing this idea of "fierce grace" with my therapist, and she helped me go a little further. "You know," she said, "St. Theresa of Lisieux's most famous quote don't you?"

She knew I had a connection to St Theresa of the Little Flowers, another name of this humble French nun who died young in the late nineteenth century. It was her statue I'd rescued from the horrible house I burned down.

I shook my head. I didn't know St. Theresa's most famous quote.

My therapist's smile widened.

"Everything is grace."

In May, 2004, my second son, Noah, was born. He and his mom also had "incompatible blood." Noah's jaundice was so severe that he had to spend his first night under therapeutic lights, apart from his mother. I sat with him until morning as he lay in the light box, my enormous hand enveloping his, listening to Nora Jones' haunting first album— "Come Away with Me," "Don't Know Why," "The Nearness of You"— over and over.

A couple of days later, I was walking with Noah through town so his mother could get some sleep. I was holding him in my arms as I wandered into a church and gazed up at the big stained-glass window shining in the sun, deep reds and oceanic blues. Jesus stood at the center, holding a lamb in his arms, much as I was holding Noah, and he was surrounded by humans and animals, all looking at him beseechingly, just as children gaze at their mothers. It hit me that Jesus was Mom! And so was Buddha. The big "miracle" here was simply that they were men who loved as mothers did, with open arms and without conditions. That was the huge breakthrough, the mindblowing accomplishment, worthy of founding entire religions! Men who were mothers.

It is said in many traditions that if you take a step toward God, He will take ten steps toward you. In the two years after we "met" Maharaj-ji, Tracey and I took several steps toward him. Tracey increasingly immersed herself in kirtan, a Hindu tradition of call-and-response singing, and yoga. I read deeply from sacred texts in the Vedic tradition and began a serious meditation practice, sitting for forty-five minutes twice a day. In October, 2005, in return, He took a big step toward us, or, actually, two steps.

The first involved the visit of a psychiatrist I had seen when I lived in Brooklyn. We had mutual friends and he had stayed in touch by phone, calling me very year or two to see how I was doing. Shortly after I had been so affected by watching *Ram Dass: Fierce Grace*, he called and asked me what was new. All I could talk about was this life-changing video. I told him he should watch it. I was saying this to everybody.

A year later, he called back and asked if he could visit us in Vermont. This felt a little weird. Whoa, dude! Like, you were my shrink and now you want to stay in my house? However, I made polite noises, saying vaguely that that would be fine, figuring nothing would come of it.

But something did. It took another year, but he came to stay with us. The first night he sat down and said, "I have to tell you why I came. You see, you changed my life."

He went on to tell me how he had watched the first twenty minutes of *Ram Dass: Fierce Grace,* and then shut it off. "I couldn't stand it." But, the following Monday, when the first of his analysis patients came in, something caught his attention. His first patient, whom he saw several times a week, was an older woman, born in Vienna before the war, very formal. About ten minutes into the session, she remarked, "Dr. Alpert, there is something different about you." Aside from the fact that this wasn't true, she had never, through years of analysis, ever made a personal observation of this kind. He did his best to reassure her, that he was still the "same old Dr. Alpert," but she wouldn't have it. Finally, just to get the session back on track, he agreed that something must be different.

However, his next session went differently as well. And the one after that, and the one after that. No other patients made personal observations, but each session had an effortless and flowing quality that he had to admit was out of the ordinary. Returning home that evening, he poured over his calendar—the typical Day-Timer of a busy New York professional, every hour accounted for. The only thing he had done differently the previous weekend was watch twenty minutes of a documentary he hated.

He sat down and watched *Ram Dass: Fierce Grace* all the way through. He got through the hard part—a section where Ram Dass counseled a couple after the tragic death of their twelve year old daughter, a girl with an uncanny resemblance to his own daughter. However, as the film moved through Ram Dass's life—from his origins as a rising star Harvard psychologist, to LSD advocate with Timothy Leary, to his meeting with Maharaj-ji, to his stroke—the doctor felt a glow in his chest, a feeling that intensified every time a picture of the guru appeared.

There was something about this Maharaj-ji's face that was especially powerful. Employing a technique of stopping a video at times of intense emotion and bringing his own face into the same expression seen on screen, using a mirror to get it exactly right, he discovered that when he brought his own features into precise alignment with Maharaj-ji's— eyes half lidded, mouth in a half smile—he could recreate this chest glow at will.

"My whole practice has been transformed!" he exclaimed. "There is almost no talking and patients experience significant improvement in just a few sessions. I have my patients put a hand on their heart center and sink into that feeling." Seeing the sparkle in his eyes, hearing the enthusiasm in his voice, I could feel that his life had indeed changed. But I had nothing to do with it.

He then taught me the essence of his new approach: simply place your hand over your heart center (middle of chest, between nipple line and clavicle) and leave it there. My experience of this technique, used in meditation, was a distinct heart opening: a concentration of warm, even glowing, energy in my heart. Through my former psychiatrist, Maharaj-ji had given me a powerful new meditation technique.

The doctor felt the same eagerness to share this good news that Tracey and I did. He bought a carton of DVDs and handed them out to friends and acquaintances. He got exactly the same responses we did: "I fell asleep"; "That Ram Dass is very self-centered;" "I couldn't get into it;" "It was interesting."

"But," he said, "I did get one unusual reaction—from my mother. She called me up right after watching it and said, 'I know that old man.' Of course, it's wall to wall old men so I asked her which one she meant."

"That George Alpert, Ram Dass's father. He's your great uncle." Until that moment, my psychiatrist, whose last name is also Alpert, had not known Ram Dass was his cousin.

The next big step Maharaj-ji took toward us occurred the day after Dr. Alpert left. Tracey and I were hosting a monthly drumming circle at our yurt and, in addition to the usual shamanic "fellow travellers," two women arrived whom we had never seen before. As we formed a circle around the central altar—a piece of fabric on which people could place objects such as feathers, crystals, carvings of power animals— one of the new women remarked on the small statue of Hanuman, the Hindu monkey god and avatar of selfless devotion. Tracey had placed him there in honor of Maharaj-ji, who many believed was Hanuman.

Other people, familiar with shamanism and knowing nothing of Hindu gods, asked who Hanuman was. Before Tracey or I could answer, the woman pulled off her sweatshirt to reveal a tight red tank top featuring Hanuman flying across her breasts. But what caught my eye was the tattoo of Maharaj-ji on her left bicep. Having a picture of one's guru was something I had heard of. But to carve him into your arm? It seemed a little over the top.

Introducing herself as Lalita Karoli ("Maharaj-ji, Neem Karoli Baba, is my true father."), she went on to tell us about Hanuman, the perfect devotee, and her husband, Kabir (named by Maharaj-ji himself) who had sat with the guru for several years in India in the early 70's.

Afterward, Tracey and I talked about the tattoo. Both of us were deeply impressed, though also a little disturbed. This was a level of devotion we were unfamiliar with.

In the months following, Tracey and I made several trips to visit Lalita and Kabir, who lived a couple of hours away. Their house was more of a temple than an ordinary home. What would have been the living room in anyone else's house was a shrine to Maharaj-ji. A huge photograph of him dominated one wall, surrounded by murtis (sacred statues) of various Hindu gods and goddesses. Meditation cushions were scattered across the floor and every meal began with an offering of food to the guru. It was as if we had been peering at him through binoculars and, all of a sudden, he had leapt into our immediate field of view. Here were people whose lives revolved around him, who had known him personally.

Six months later, Lalita was visiting our house. It was my birthday and I was reminded of her tattoo. I asked her to show it to me. "Do you mean this one?" she asked, pulling her shirt back to reveal a wolf on her shoulder blade. "No, no, " I said, laughing. "The one of Maharaj-ji." She gave me a blank look. "This is my only tattoo." I figured she was teasing me. "No, no. The one on your left bicep." Again, the blank look as she pulled her sleeve back to reveal bare skin. There was no tattoo.

It is hard to describe what the guru feels like. I tried to get Kabir to explain it one time. After all, he had been one of the first Americans to make contact with Maharaj-ji, had spent several years with him. The closest he could get was saying that the guru was like an enormous dynamo, radiating love in a huge circumference, like the sun. I nodded. The fact he had died when I was a boy didn't seem to make any difference. I could feel it, too.

Krishna Das, a well-known Maharaj-ji devotee and kirtan performer, says it's like taking everyone you've ever been in love with and rolling all those feelings together into a big ball. It's something like that, he says. Only bigger.

For me, Maharaj-ji made me see and feel my heart in my chest, like a big golden bird, soaring and nesting at the same time. He made everything feel as if it were going to be all right. He put me in touch with a love that was completely impersonal, which is to say that this love did not require anything from me. I didn't have to be good or smart or hardworking or nice. I was loved exactly as I was. As Ram Dass said in the documentary, "He knew everything about me, all my good thoughts and my bad ones, and he still loved me."

Maharaj-ji even touched our four year old daughter, Maia. He appeared in one of her dreams, his face huge and shining, like a great sun on the horizon. But it was how he came through her that most affected me.

I went into the kitchen one morning and she came up to me, took my hand and looked straight into my eyes. "Daddy, I an artist." As I stared into her blue eyes, I wasn't looking at a little girl. There was a tone in her voice, a power in her stare, that did not have any age at all. Cute as this scene was on the surface, it was not remotely like that. These words came from very, very deep in my daughter, from a place no younger or older than me. And her tone, her look, made it very clear that I would ignore them at my peril.

She then held up a picture she had made with crayons. It was the outline of her hand in red, with each finger colored in differently—yellow, pine, pink, gray, grass green. And each one represented a different realm, she told me: sunny summer, foggy day, pink world, frosty winter, spring. The palm was Mother Earth. I was reminded of a story about Maharaj-ji's most famous mudra, hand position: index finger extended as if in admonition. He could make this gesture at any time and when he did, all conversation would stop.

One of his devotees asked him what he meant. Was he angry, impatient, trying to make a point? Maharaj-ji just looked at the man and made the gesture, index finger raised up like a ball bat. But then, he raised each of his other fingers, one by one, until he was holding up all five, just like in my daughter's drawing. He then closed his fingers into a fist and raised just the index finger once more. "Sub ek," he said. All one. And this was his essential teaching: that whatever we might be thinking or seeing or talking about, IT was all One, the core message of the ancient Hindu philosophical school, Advaita Vedanta.

And here, in my four year old daughter's crayon drawing, was the same teaching: that all in one hand, even the tiny hand of a little girl, were held many worlds, many realities. Sub ek. All one.

Chapter 9

SHIP4707

Tracey and I were on fire for the guru, just as when we first met, we had been on fire for shamanism. And, just as it had been with journeying, with Maharaj-ji guiding our lives, everything seemed possible.

We weren't journeying much anymore. We continued to offer the shamanic teaching program, *Seeing With the Heart*; the course title was a traditional definition of what a shaman does. But, personally, our power animals and spirit teachers had been largely replaced by Maharaj-ji. When you have the guru, you don't need to journey anywhere. He is always right where you are. Even though I hadn't really known what it meant to "see with the heart" when we named our course, that's really what we were doing now. Using the drum felt more and more like training wheels after you know how to ride a bicycle.

When Tracey and I had met, we journeyed on everything: our path together, where we should live, what we should do next. Our motto was "Journey on it!" And, because the information you receive in a shamanic journey is so metaphorical, each journey usually required more journeys to clarify it.

One day, early on in our relationship, Tracey was told in a journey we were to live "on 707." There was a Route 707 near where we she lived. Maybe this was where we were supposed to live. I went to Kentucky to visit her soon after and we set off to explore this mythical road.

In our minds, we saw some kind of paradise where we could settle and heal the world. However, this was Appalachia. The road was lined with ramshackle trailer homes and collapsing barns. By the end of our tour, we knew we would not be living on Route 707.

However, when we finally found our dream home, burned it down, and built a new one, the computer-generated password given to us by our internet provider was SHIP4707. Ship for 707. Head for 707. So it was some kind of destination. The trail ended there in 1999. We had too many other things to think about.

So when 2007 rolled around, we were no longer thinking about what 707 might mean. We were too busy grappling with what marriage can reveal.

The best definition of marriage I know of comes from *Constructing the Sexual Crucible*, the title itself an explanation of what marriage really does. Marriage, according to author, couples counselor David Schnarch, is a "people-growing machine." We may get hitched because we believe we have finally found "true love" or our "soul mate" or some other pretty notion, but the fact is that marriage is the most effective way to get people to grow and evolve that has ever been discovered.

As Schnarch points out, the transformational mystery of marriage is that each partner is trying to change the other, consciously or unconsciously. At the same time, each partner must make some of these changes if she is to grow and remain married and, also must not make certain changes if she is to maintain her personal integrity. Threading this needle, walking this razor's edge, is the "crucible," the purifier, of each partner.

So, while our shared love for shamanism brought Tracey and me together, following that bliss brought us right up against our souls' true purposes, which often comes as a complete surprise. At first, the fact that we both felt strongly called by Maharaj-ji felt like a miraculous coincidence, further evidence of our "divinely" blessed union. Usually, we thought, only one person in the couple hears that call and is pulled away from the one who doesn't. How lucky for us.

However, just because the Guru had called both of us did not mean he had the same plans for Tracey and me. The inspiration Tracey felt from Maharaj-ji directed her to more passionately follow her love for music and yoga. Kirtan and vinyasa yoga became her calling.

However, for me, Maharaj-ji's enlightenment was the example I was drawn to; the freedom he had found. And while yoga (Sanskrit for both "union" and "yoke") was clearly the way, the "yoga" I was drawn to, the original astanga (eight limbed) yoga of Patanjali, had very little to do with singing or asanas (postures). What Patanjali literally said in his legendary Yoga Sutras was "sit and breathe." And, while you are at it, for God's sake, stop thinking!

Study and meditation became my core practice. I arose each morning at five to read the words of enlightened masters and, so focused, I would meditate for at least thirty minutes. If time permitted, I would climb the ridge behind our house and meditate there for half an hour or an hour in the afternoon. Meditating outside, seated on a rock or under a tree, was my new bliss.

So off we went, each following our new coordinates, our new joy, each with our own understanding of what yoga meant. We still taught *Seeing With the Heart* classes together every weekend, we both still taught adjunct classes at local colleges, but it only took a couple of years before we could barely understand each other.

By 2007, Tracey was immersed in recording original songs and kirtans. She was working with a sound engineer I had gone to college with and had recommended to her. What I did not know was that this man loved to make women fall in love with him. Luke didn't want to sleep with them; he was still under his own guru's command after all. But he just couldn't help seducing them into adoring him. Tracey was no exception.

This was a huge experience for her. Although her musical gifts had been apparent since childhood, this was her first experience bringing them into public view. Luke, a gifted professional musician himself, was the perfect midwife for her gifts. Spiritual and empathic, he guided Tracey to bring out the best in her music. Not surprising, she began to fall in love with him. And, being the uber honest Sagittarius she was, she lost no time in telling me about it.

She was clear: she had no intention of leaving me or sleeping with him. However, she admitted, there was an undeniable infatuation that was increasing as the recording process went on. This was kryptonite for me. Tracey was making her attraction (and its limitations) clear, but all I could feel was the knife twisting.

As the recording sessions continued through the winter, my jealousy increased, culminating with my discovery of emails about how they needed to get together to see where this new relationship was going. This was the last straw. Tracey was married to me! There should be no ambiguity whatsoever about where any relationship with another man could go.

I printed the emails up and confronted her, waving the pages like a lawyer cross-examining a hostile witness. My reaction was so angry, so over the top, that Tracey became angry and defensive, not the least bit apologetic. "You're acting as if I had already slept with him! We are just trying to get clear. And what were you doing reading my emails anyway?"

Neither of us would back down. She went on to have that meeting where they acknowledged the mutual attraction as well as the fact that they were both married and had children. They recognized that this kind of attraction happens from time to time, even in the best marriages, and that they would not act on their feelings.

However, this did little to assuage my suspicions or, more to the point, my wounded ego. Luke starred in a realm where I had little to no talent. This realm was clearly where Tracey wanted to go and I had little to offer except support. I was certainly never going to be the object of her adoration here.

I spiraled down into depression and self-pity. To make matters worse, Luke took it upon himself to become my confidant as well. As he guided Tracey to bring out her talents, he steered me toward a charismatic evangelical minister who spoke in tongues and laid on hands. I was desperate enough that I went along.

Meanwhile, Shiloh, a friend from the Harner program came to visit. One of the most remarkable things about this program was watching how it affected people. Because shamanism has no doctrine, no rules (except perhaps the idea that "everything that is is alive"), its techniques allow whatever is inside a person to come out. As the ninety or so of us worked together for three years (and beyond), it was a little like watching each of our idiosyncrasies being fed Miracle-Gro.

Shiloh, although outwardly resembling a blonde, bubbly Colorado soccer mom, defied expectation. Her spirit guide, who had inspired her to travel to Africa to study with shamans there, was an old black man who "threw the bones," divined with a set of specially acquired animal bones. Entering a trance, Shiloh would take on this man's mannerisms as she cast and then interpreted her small bag of sacred objects, the original dice.

Seeing what a bad way I was in, she offered to throw the bones for me. Hell, if I was willing to meet with Luke's minister, I was certainly willing to hear what Shiloh had to say. We went out into the woods. She called in the directions and then cast her bones on the ground. Her eyes faraway, her words hoarse and accented, she was no longer a suburban housewife. Closing my eyes, I could see an old African man and I listened to his words, "This sickness that is upon you is from long ago, from before you were born. No human will be able to lift it from you. Only the ancestors, the nature spirits, can lift it from you. You must go into the lodge for one...No, two...No, Three! Three days! Three days!"

Gradually her voice died away and she came back to herself. After a few moments, she asked cheerfully, "So? What did I say?"

"He, you, said I needed to do a three-day sweat lodge."

There was silence as she contemplated these words.

"I am so sorry."

Three hours in a lodge, if it's hot enough, can put you in the hospital, even kill you. Three *days* in a lodge? I had never heard of such a thing.

After Shiloh left, I had a lot to think about. However, things were not getting better with my marriage or my mood. Every time Tracey went to a recording session with Luke, my cruel mind tormented itself with images of their closeness.

I decided to go for it. I found a team of male friends to support me. One would come every four hours to stoke the fire and replenish the stones. It would really be a modified vision quest: three days of silence and fasting, but in complete darkness. There was an important difference—I could drink as much water as I wanted. I would otherwise die from dehydration.

And so for three days, I sat, kneeled, lay, and prayed in the darkness. Lying on a bearskin, I called over and over for this sickness, this malaise to be lifted from me. For this depression, this jealousy, this self-loathing to go for good.

The only time I saw daylight was when the lodge flap was lifted for more stones to be brought in or to go out to urinate. Standing outside peeing, at the halfway point, listening to the rustle of wind in the leaves, birdsong from the branches, it occurred to me that this moment—alone, hungry, outside—was a typical moment on an ordinary vision quest. However, after having been confined in a small, dark, hot space for hours, the relief of being outside felt like liberation.

By the third day, it began to smell like something had died. I couldn't tell if it was me or the bearskin. This couldn't continue much longer. However, words began to come into my mind, slowly, at intervals.

Held. I was held here.

Healed. I was healed here.

Whole. I was whole.

Holy. Very holy.

And, finally,

Home. I was home.

Not just now, but always.

The following month, July, 2007, I met my living guru, Amritanandamayi, "the Mother of Immortal Bliss," known as Amma (Mom) or "the hugging saint." Born in 1953 as Sudhamani Idamannel, Amma grew up poor in a small fishing village in the southwest of India. As the darkest of her siblings (and therefore the least marriageable), she was pulled out of school after the fourth grade and rented out to relatives. For a small monthly fee, she became a household servant of virtual strangers who could treat her as they pleased.

115

However, her single-pointed commitment to God showed itself early. From the age of three, the young Sudhamani was often found in deep meditation or composing and singing bhajans (sacred songs) to Krishna that she had composed herself. Her family and neighbors attributed this unusual behavior to some sort of mental illness. The irony is that, had Amma grown up in more "privileged" circumstances, she would have undoubtedly been sent to mental health professionals, possibly put into an institution, and certainly medicated. In Kerala, where she grew up, however, she was largely left on her own, regarded as hopeless.

When she came of age and her parents began to look for possible husbands, ideally from far enough away that they would not have heard the stories, she made it clear she intended never to marry. The third time her parents brought a potential suitor to the house, she emerged from the kitchen brandishing a large knife and chased the man out of the house. After that, there was no more talk of marriage.

Her behavior became more bizarre. When neighbors had readings from sacred Hindu texts in their yard (a South Indian equivalent of an American barbeque combined with church), she would come uninvited, striking poses associated with Krishna. Again, while some people saw this as more craziness, there is a tradition in India of people channeling divine beings on occasion and her neighbors saw her actions as enhancing their experience.

People began to ask her to perform a miracle. Again, in India, it is widely believed that people possessed by a divine being can display magical powers such as performing healings or producing objects out of thin air. After several more weeks of such demands, Amma agreed to do so the following week.

Word had spread and several hundred people were in attendance that day, eagerly awaiting whatever might happen. Some were truly devout, others merely curious, and there was also a band of committed "rationalists" eager to see her fail.

116

Amma asked the host to fill a copper pot with water and bring it to her. He did and she held it for a moment before handing it back.

"Tell the people what is in the pot," she commanded.

"Milk," the startled man responded.

She then gestured for him to give the pot back to her. She again held the pot and then returned it to the host.

"Now tell them."

The astonished man dipped his finger in and pulled it out covered with a sweet pudding, said to be the boy Krishna's favorite treat.

"Now let all who wish have a taste."

The small pot passed slowly among the crowd as each person looked in and gasped, often putting in a finger to make sure. By the end of the display, over a hundred people had received a taste.

What makes this story different from, say, the miracle stories of Jesus, is that this event occurred in 1970. Over half the people in attendance that day are still alive, many with college degrees, all eager to share startling similar accounts of the mysterious event. The host himself is proudest of all and has kept the pot in a place of honor in his family puja room for decades.

Disciples began to gather around Amma, including many young Indian men with college or advanced degrees. These men's families were uniformly horrified that their sons were being led astray by this humble "fisher girl" and some even resorted to kidnapping in attempts to "deprogram" their captivated sons.

The local villagers were not much happier. That a single woman should be consorting with young men at all hours of the day and night was scandalous. Amma's parents commanded their daughter to cease such embarrassing behavior.

To no avail. Amma converted the family cowshed to a small temple space and registered the property as a legal ashram. As her followers grew in numbers, they quickly outgrew their humble quarters. There was no money to buy or build a larger building. Instead she pointed to the shallow lagoon bordering her parents' small property. "Let there be a temple here," she instructed, pointing to the water. At first her devotees were puzzled, but soon shovels and wheelbarrows were obtained and so began the slow and laborious job of hauling dirt from around the village and filling the lagoon.

Donations began to pour in and her ashram began to take shape. However, Amma's behavior continued to provoke outrage. Because she saw herself, literally, as the mother of all who appeared before her, she manifested her message of unconditional love in the clearest way she knew how: she hugged everyone. Not only are Indians not big huggers, but for a young unmarried woman to embrace every stranger who comes to her is just shy of becoming a prostitute. Outrage grew commensurate with her following.

The goodwill and joy that radiated from those drawn to her was inarguable. It was not long before she began to channel such positivity into *seva* or selfless service. Projects to feed, educate and house the poor flowered. Before long, an enormous temple in the shape of a lotus sprouted from the filled lagoon area and colleges and hospitals grew up in her name.

In 1987, Amma began the first of the annual world tours which continue to this day. At this point, she has literally hugged tens of millions of people, often for eight, ten, twelve hours at a time without a bathroom or meal break, along the way raising millions of dollars for her many charities.

The story about Amma that stays with me is the account of Dattan, the leper. Although leprosy is easily cured with antibiotics and thus virtually unknown in America, in places where people cannot afford medicine, leprosy is still a serious health issue. Across India, among the poor, a diagnosis of leprosy means exile. A leper's family will kick him out. He will no longer be welcome in his village and no one will hire him. A diagnosis of leprosy is often to be sentenced to a life of wandering and begging as one's body slowly rots.

Dattan's leprosy was so bad not even other lepers would associate with him. His disease was so advanced, the percentage of his flesh that was decomposing so great, that people were overwhelmed by the smell. Because many lepers survive by begging, they must at least get close enough to passers-by that they can make their needs known. But because Dattan's leprosy was so extensive, his smell became unbearable to anyone coming within twenty or thirty yards of him. The stench of Dattan from a close distance could make people vomit.

Dattan heard about Amma, this saint who saw herself as everyone's mother. Surely such a one would not shun him. Perhaps not, but when Dattan arrived at Amma's ashram in Kerala, none of the people at the gates wanted anything to do with him. He was told in no uncertain terms to get lost. However, for Dattan, this was his last chance, his last hope for any kind of help. He persisted, refused to leave. Soon there was yelling and shouting, an uproar.

Amma herself came to the gates to see what was wrong. Her devotees lost no time in telling her of this horrible man who had come to befoul the ashram. Surely she would make him see he was not welcome?

"All who come here are my children," responded Amma. "Bring him to me."

The devotees reluctantly formed an opening in their throng and pointed Dattan to Amma. Upon seeing him, her eyes welled with tears. She opened her arms. "Oh, my poor child," she murmured, embracing him. "Come with me."

Amma then led Dattan to the main temple. Although many devotees were too sickened by the sight and smell of this man to follow, several dozen came into the temple as well. Many wished they had not.

Amma proceeded to lick Dattan's puss-dripping sores with her tongue, dabbing at them with a cloth. This procedure continued for hours and was captured on film by an American devotee. In the clip, which can be seen on Youtube, we watch as this tiny woman licks a much taller man all over his body, much as a cat would bathe a kitten, repeated small licks and bobs of the head. What the film does not reveal is how many members of the audience were throwing up in response.

While leprosy is not highly contagious, like AIDs it is spread through bodily fluids. If a person wanted to contract leprosy, Amma was providing an excellent demonstration of how this could be done. However, after several sessions, not only did Amma not contract leprosy, but Dattan was completely healed. A picture of him, taken sometime after this event, shows the deep pock marks all over his face, but what catches one's attention are his eyes: there is an expression there of such depth, such compassion, such gratitude and peace. This is the expression of one who has seen, directly experienced, a kind of love most of us could not imagine. This is a man who has seen God, knows how much She loves him.

I first heard about Amma from Sandra Ingerman, who was still an important teacher for me. Sandra told stories of the saint drinking poison and being unaffected because she knew so deeply that *everything* was God. Lalita, the Maharaj-ji devotee who burst into our lives a couple of years earlier, had actually been to see her and told us that many of Maharaj-ji's followers had become Amma devotees as well because of her extraordinary power and love. Still, I was a Maharaj-ji loyalist and meditated at his altar twice a day. There could only be one guru for me.

120

At one of Sandra's workshops in 2006, the woman who had been sitting on my left and the woman who had been sitting on my right each gave me gifts they had received from Amma—a picture and a necklace—separately and without having spoken to each other. I didn't think much of this coincidence at the time. Maharaj-ji was my guy. I figured they were gifts for Tracey, who had taken an interest in Amma, and passed them along to her.

A couple of months later, Tracey went by herself to meet Amma, when the guru was visiting in the US. I stayed at home to watch the kids. Just the same, as I watched the sun set that evening, an enormous orange disk peering at me through the mist, I felt something was happening. I just didn't know what.

The next day, when Tracey returned, she was completely lit up. As she recounted each moment of the experience—waiting in the crowd for Amma to arrive, watching and feeling her entry into the convention hall, standing in line, the hug itself— I hung on every word. Just as people described the extraordinary energy coming from Ram Dass after he returned from India, having just met Maharaj-ji for the first time, I could feel the transmission of love, an enormous shining, pouring out of Tracey. I knew I would be going to see Amma next year.

In 2007, I finally met Amma. The guru, in a body! This moment is legendary in the annals of devotional literature. One of the greatest blessings a person can receive is that they might meet their guru in this lifetime. All of Rumi's poetry sings of this experience. The Beloved is the guru! The dispeller of darkness. The one who shows you the truth.

The western mind goes nuts with this. "Whaddya mean 'show me the truth'?" the ego snorts. "I already know the truth." Guru-related scandals pour into the mind. Skepticism and doubt yell their protests. Everything we have been taught tells us we are on thin ice. Danger! Here is where we have to hit the pause button and switch to feelings.

Think of how you felt about Santa Claus when you first believed in him. Think about the first time you fell in love. The feeling in your heart is golden. You know in your body this is real. Your joy spilling over tells you this. The smile on your lips tells you this. The air in the room is thick with it. The incredible lightness that suffuses your body, that shines out of the hundreds of people around you, tells you this.

And this is what it feels like to be with Amma. Many of the two or three thousand people present were wearing white, a sign of respect for the guru. At least half the crowd were Indians of all ages, many with children. My actual hug wouldn't be for hours. Each of us had a token, indicating when our turn would come. Hundreds of people were ahead of me. Just the same, I already felt held. Even though the room was packed and noisy—countless conversations, Amma's bhajan band wailing—I felt a delicious sense of peace, as if I were floating in joy. And all this came from just being in the same room with her.

Watching her up on the stage, surrounded by swamis in orange, assistants in white, two long lines of devotees snaking up to her from opposite sides of the hall, my eyes kept returning to the stillpoint, the endlessly recurring hug at the center of it all. Most of the hugs only lasted a few seconds, the devotee kneeling before Amma, a tiny dark figure all in white, whose hands kept rising up like a bird's wings, to enfold the devotee in front of her. And even though the process was unceasing and repetitive, an assembly line of love, each embrace was unique.

With some, Amma was all laughs, and, with others deeply concerned. Some she whispered to for a second, but, with a few, the hugs seemed endless. Time would stop as she held the person in an embrace that continued for many seconds. Her attention simultaneously poured into the person before her and also to the crowd around her, each of whom needed something.

It went on for hours. The hugs started in late morning and continued through the afternoon. Amma never took a break. Never even sat back to take a breath. Just an endless outflow of attention. Hours of unconditional love. And it would start up again that evening and go on for even longer, often continuing until after sunrise.

Sitting there, waiting for my hug, I was watching the Buddha, seeing Jesus, in real time. Right there before my eyes was unconditional love—love for every single person who came before her regardless of who they were or what they might have done. No one was turned away. No one had to pay a dime. Everyone who came before her was embraced. This love, this joy—she never stopped smiling and laughing and joking—was constant, unstoppable, and radiated out over everyone in the enormous hall. It wasn't just the person getting the hug. We all felt it.

But what gobsmacked me was that Amma is an actual human being. What she is doing, then, is humanly possible. Amma is so clearly flesh and blood, like us! When she hugged me, I saw the bruise on her cheek from hundreds of previous embraces. Even though it was July, she was wearing Smartwool socks to keep her feet warm. Her voice, hoarse from countless conversations and lectures, day after day, was sweet and high-pitched, like a bird. And her expressions moved like a bird, too, smiling, then concerned, then quizzical.

Someone once asked Amma what it felt like to be adored by so many people. She looked at them, puzzled. "Adoring me? No, no. I am adoring them!" And that's her secret. We come to her, our heads filled with all kinds of misconceptions—I am unworthy; I am flawed; I have so far to go; I wish she would give me something. And, all the while, she looks at us with a clear knowing of what we actually are: no different from her. As our mother, she knows who we are, what we are capable of.

And this is why so many spiritual traditions say the guru is necessary for enlightenment, for true liberation. Because we are mammals. Because we are hardwired to develop fully only at the breast of another. The baby who is not nursed, or at least held closely, can never become a normal child, cannot develop the responses and abilities necessary to interact in a healthy way with his fellows. The mammalian dyad—baby at the mother's breast—is a brief but necessary moment in the individual's evolution.

In its first iteration, this dyad occurs only between mother and child. But in a highly complex species—like us—capable of many developmental leaps, this dyadic relationship must be repeated as many times as the individual wishes to evolve. Teacher-student. Coach-athlete. Mentor-mentee. Therapist-patient. Each time, we need someone ahead of us to show that it can be done, to hold us safely as we overcome our fears and misconceptions about what lies ahead. Monkey see—monkey do.

At this point in human history, the mass of humans have only evolved through the first three chakras, Sanskrit for "wheel," the energy centers that progress up through the body from root to crown, a little like Maslow's hierarchy of needs. These first three chakras—roughly corresponding to survival, sexuality and personal power—are the lowest common denominators of human evolution.

Think of the movies you watch, the political debates that rage, the narrative of the news. What holds our attention the most? Survival, sexuality and power. The fourth chakra, the heart chakra—our ability to love—might show up on a small scale, in families or intimate friendships, but it certainly has not entered the collective conversation. Think of the reaction to Marianne Williamson's brief run for president.

The developmental threshold that humans are at now in history is called, in yoga, the Vishnu granthi, "knot," the naturally occurring hurdle between the third and fourth chakras. It shows up physiologically as the diaphragm, the thin skeletal muscle that sits at the base of the chest and separates the abdomen from the chest. We feel it energetically as fear, the unwillingness to become vulnerable.

124

Even though billions may call themselves "Christians," the most common representation of Christ—on the cross—represents in practical terms the same kind of crude warning you might see at a dangerous intersection or on a toxic product: this is what could happen to you if you are not careful.

There are so many who profess a faith in Jesus, but how many of these have the slightest intention of doing what He did? And, of course, that huge warning sign, available in every artistic style you can imagine, is the simple answer. Who in his right mind wants to be tortured for hours while he is mocked by his community and then nailed onto a cross through his hands and feet?

What we don't realize, not most of us, is that this image, like the image of Kali, the Hindu goddess of destruction— dark blue skin, tongue lolling, wearing a necklace of skulls—is only how the ego sees it. This image is what it feels like to have all our ideas about ourselves, all the conceptions we armor ourselves with, removed so that the heart can really do what it's supposed to do: love. This is what happened when Richard Alpert felt his heart crack open when Maharaj-ji said "spleen." This is what happened to me when I looked into my first wife's eyes and realized how terribly I had betrayed her. It is what anyone feels when they realize, at a deep level, they are not who they thought they were.

And who we think we are is what it's all about in a world ruled by the first three chakras, by the ego, by the mind. All the walls and guns and insulating layers we put up to protect ourselves and the stuff— possessions and mental concepts—that defines us. It's all gotta go if we want to be free. But who in his right mind would ever agree to that, could ever find the willingness to do that? And just as mammals require a mother to help them on that hard, slow journey from fetus to child, humans need a guru, a dispeller of darkness, if they want to find a way from living in the bomb shelter of the first three chakras to breathing the clear open air of unconditional love.

Because the heart is the fulcrum of the whole business. When you have nailed three out of seven chakras, you are batting .420, pretty good for baseball. Who wants to risk it all just to get to the heart, which is mushy and soft and no help in a street fight? What we don't realize, can't imagine because we have never been there, is that fully entering the heart chakra—feeling love for everything that is—is the hard work. At that point you are four out of seven. The next three chakras— the throat, third eye, and crown— will open naturally, of their own accord, like a flower blossoming.

It's just like the biggest hurdle in the life of the germ of a seed. Remember, when we say "seed," we are talking about the shell that is only a protective layer, worthless in the long run. The money shot is when the germ breaks out. Once that happens, the root goes down, the leaf goes up, and the mighty oak is on her way. "But that's very dangerous," I hear you say. "Most seeds don't ever germinate. And many of the ones who do, die soon afterward."

And again, this is why the guru is necessary: a loving gardener, someone to help the seed when it is ready to emerge; someone to watch over the new plant and help it find its way until it can fend for itself. As mammals, we have the mother.

And of all human mammals, a few have gone past the third chakra— think of Buddha, Jesus, Maharaj-ji, Amma. But the rest of us, stuck in the first three, collectively are killing the world.

To save this world, we must take the great leap to love. We must stay in one place, even more vulnerable than our earliest sedentary ancestors were when surrounded by prowling nomads, and crack open our tightly bound hearts, for so long safely encased in the shell of ego, the mind, and who it tells us we are, what it tells us the world is.

126

Back in the hall, I waited in a short line at the side of the stage to receive my mantra. I had already gone up on the stage to receive my hug, so fast and overwhelming I could barely recall it, but getting a mantra is a very special moment in the life of the devotee. Mantras, or prayers, can be found in any book or across the internet, but to have these words poured into your ear, impregnated in your heart, by the guru is a sacred initiation. This act links you to this special, once-in-many-lifetimes teacher and, when followed by constant repetition, can set you free. It is like the "egg tooth," the small, sharp, cranial protuberance found in birds which allows the offspring to break through the egg's surface during hatching. If you say it enough times and with enough devotion, the mantra will break through the shell of the ego and set you free.

My turn came. Amma leaned over and whispered the sacred words into my left ear. She then kissed me on the forehead and returned to her endless hugs. I came off the stage in a daze and went to sit along the side of the hall and practice my new mantra.

It was July, 2007. I had finally arrived at 7/07.

Chapter 10

What Comes Next

After a month of repeating the sacred words Amma had given me, Tracey and I were on the rocks. She was continuing to record with Luke and it was eating me up. "Can't you see how much pain this is causing me?" I pleaded.

"I am sick of your pain."

She had some reason to be. Luke didn't come out of nowhere. I had also fallen in love with someone else, a student from one of our workshops, a beautiful twenty-something named Kiera. We had an extraordinary connection. I became a mentor for her and she saw, appreciated aspects of me no one else did. I guided her on a vision quest and when she headed home afterward, I was heartbroken. She felt like a childhood best friend, that one person in the world you can really be yourself with.

A year before Tracey started recording with Luke, I had gone to visit Kiera one night, poured my heart out to her. We started to kiss and then it became very clear what a terrible idea this was. I stopped it, talked it through, but I had crossed a line.

This had happened before. These kinds of feelings and what they can lead to had wrecked my first marriage. I immediately went into therapy and got a new twelve-step sponsor. After six months of therapy, I got up the nerve to tell Tracey. I knew, from how I had devastated Nancy with a flood of specific details, how damaging too much truth can be.

I decided to err on the side of caution. I told of the visit to Kiera, my intent, but I did not mention the kiss. No need to hurt Tracey with gratuitous details.

We got through it, went on with our marriage, but a month or two after, Kiera called to inquire about one of our events. She was still one of our students. Tracey answered the phone. Kiera was clearly flustered, and asked Tracey, "Did he tell you that we kissed?" And that was it. Our marriage was beyond repair.

It's funny the things you don't see at the time. It was just a kiss. We didn't go any further. I was never alone with Kiera again. But for Tracey, hearing that question—"Did he tell you that we kissed?"—and not having known, but hearing it from this much younger woman— and knowing I had shared this secret with this woman. That was hard to come back from. The kind of small wound that might heal over on the surface, but remains infected, becomes gangrenous over time.

The signs were subtle at first, but I did notice Tracey flirting more with other men. She had never lacked for admirers before I came along. It became more obvious with a man who assisted us with summer camps. Their shared jokes, long gazes, began to make me uncomfortable. When I finally brought it up, Tracey brushed it off. "Oh, it's nothing. It's not like we ever kissed."

And then came Luke. It's striking how we intuit our partner's weakest spots. I had cut Tracey at her deepest place and, in return, she cut me at mine. We staggered along like this, each quietly bleeding inside, for another four years. In the meantime, we continued trying to walk together. We had too much invested, inextricably woven, to make it easy to go our separate ways.

I told her I was going to move out, then changed my mind. And then it was her turn. "You have to go." I had heard this before, from Nancy, but this time I wasn't leaving. So we compromised. We agreed that I would move into the smaller yurt, the one we had first lived in while building the dome. I would continue to help care for the kids, take some meals together, but for the next year I would be sleeping under another roof. The retreat with my new mantra had begun.

My first memory is of waking up alone in a crib in a dark room, standing and holding the bars, screaming, and no one coming. I was two. This fear of abandonment continued for the rest of my life. Was this the terror beneath my depression? The longing manifested in addictive behavior, sending me after food, alcohol, sex, in unhealthy ways.

Most of my life, I had never wanted to delve too deeply into this memory. And now all my running, all my struggling, had me right back there. The lattice work of the yurt's interior reminded me of a giant play pen, the place where you put your crawling or toddling child when you don't want him to run amok. And now, that's where I had been put.

I went to bed alone now, woke up alone. I had a large picture of Amma on the wall and the mantra she had given me. But a lot of the time, no matter how much I cried that mantra out, nobody seemed to be coming.

It was during this time that I went with Luke to his church to meet Father Nigel. Father Nigel was an interesting guy. Born in England, his father had been an Anglican minister who laid on hands and spoke in tongues, not typical for this brand of Christianity, which was more associated with the Queen and a very stiff upper lip. But young Nigel had no interest and joined the Royal Marines instead.

While stationed in Belfast during the Troubles, he saw his best friend shot dead by an IRA sniper. The thing that really got him was this: after the body was taken away in the ambulance, several Catholic teenagers danced on the bloody patch of pavement where his best friend had died.

"It took every ounce of willpower not to lift my rifle and pull the trigger," Father Nigel confided in me one day when I had sought him out for counseling. "And then I went into a terrible depression, had to leave the Marines." It was during this time that he found Jesus. In his desperation, he would call on Christ to stand between him and his despair, to protect him from the wave of loss and self-hatred that poured over him when he thought of his friend, what he had almost done yet had not been able to do, that terrible place that threatened to take him down.

And that's what happened to me. I would sit in the front row as Nigel preached and spoke in tongues and called people up to be healed and I would call on Jesus Christ and sob. It's hard to explain how I could so completely surrender to this kind of religion that had always repelled me, but now, in my desperation, it was the one thing that helped. I would focus on the crucified figure on the wall behind Father Nigel and I would ask to be able to surrender as he had. "Father, Father, why has thou forsaken me?" These were not just words. This was the situation I was in, kicked out of the house I had built, sleeping alone in a big tent way out in the woods, attending church where the organist was the guy who had stolen my wife's affections.

After weeks of attending this church, going up to the altar for people to lay hands on me, something began to shift. I got home from teaching at the local community college one day and was the only one around. Tracey was out with the kids. Maia was six now and Noah was three. I was alone and it hit me that Tracey and I were done, that there was no coming back from this, that I had lost her. Grief welled up from deep inside, continued to build and build until it flooded my entire body. And it just kept coming. I was completely alone in this vast wilderness and no one was coming, was ever going to come. I felt as if like my head would explode and I started to scream. I ran into the forest, screaming, running and screaming until I couldn't breathe. I would stop for a moment, catch my breath, feel a moment of respite, and then the feelings would start again, rising, like when you are about to throw up. I would start to scream again, and to run, until I found myself at a small waterfall about a mile from the house. I tore off my clothes—it was November—and threw myself into the freezing water. Maybe this would take the pain away.

Standing in the pool at the bottom of the small falls, I saw a figure above me, at the lip of the pouring water. He was bearded and wrapped in a blanket. I stopped crying. He had come! And, just like that, the figure disappeared and I was alone. But this time it didn't matter. I knew Jesus was with me.

The days and weeks that followed weren't really any better in terms of how Tracey and I were getting along. We continued our excruciating sessions of couples counseling, painstakingly going over all the things that had gone wrong between us. But something had shifted. I wasn't as desperate. I still wanted to save the marriage, stay with the kids, continue the mission of Spirit Hollow, but now it didn't feel like life or death. I would be ok with whatever happened.

That spring, my friend John invited me to join him in Ireland for an unusual workshop. John was the one who held hands with me around the oak the night of the mushrooms, was one of the men who watched over me on my first vision quest and, when he decided to walk the Appalachian Trail, Tracey and I had driven him to Springer Mountain in Georgia to start the hike with him and I had met John at Katahdin to finish it. And now, as I was coming to the end of my long winter, he wanted me to come with him to take part in another extraordinary experience.

The man leading it, Michael Murphy, was a paradox: an Irish psychiatrist, a member of the ethnic group Freud famously declared immune to psychoanalysis. After many years pioneering hospice in the US, he had developed a program he termed *Love, Loss and Forgiveness*, the three stages he believed all people must go through if they truly wished to be healed, to be set free from their pain.

The workshop participants were split into into groups of three, where one would take the role of child, one was a parent, and the third would be a witness. He would then ask us to recall specific moments from childhood—when we first felt we had been abandoned, the first time we felt unseen—and to act them out. As "child," I would imagine myself back in that time of pain, say what I felt in that moment. The second person would play the role of my mother or father. The third person would just observe, a loving witness to what transpired.

The process went very deep very quickly and everyone was sobbing by the end of the second day. During this five-day workshop, held in a Tibetan Buddhist retreat center in southwestern Ireland, Michael also had us do "mirror work," where we looked at ourselves in a hand mirror after these cathartic sessions and described what we saw.

For most of my life, I did not cry. It started when I was six. I was alone in the house one day and felt terribly sad. I began to think how alone I felt, how uncared for, until I was sobbing. Feeling exquisitely sorry for myself, a delicious self-pity, I decided to look at myself in the mirror. I knew I was the picture of the most adorable tragedy. Instead, what greeted me in the mirror was a little boy with puffy red eyes, his face smeared with tears. I didn't look heartbreakingly endearing at all. I looked pathetic. I didn't cry again for fifteen years.

There was reason for this harsh self-judgment. It had been taught to me. The most dramatic lesson I can remember occurred when I was five. We were living in Kentucky, while my dad worked in the Public Health Service. My parents had rented a house on Calumet Farm, a legendary racing stable which produced multiple Triple Crown winners.

The house was a white brick mansion in a spectacular setting, right out of a magazine spread, but we were completely isolated. There were no other houses near us, just nine hundred acres of rolling bluegrass, crisp white fences, fields containing horses you couldn't go anywhere near. "Stay away from them horses, boy," a trainer told me in my first days on the farm, holding up his hand. "See this? A stallion did this to me." I stared at his hand, at the three stumps where fingers used to be.

Every day, my dad would go to work and my mom and me and my little brother, still in diapers, would rattle around the big empty house. My mom was depressed a lot and often sent me outside to play by myself, but the isolation and the demands of two small children sometimes overwhelmed her and she would explode.

I was standing in my brother's room one day, looking up at him on the changing table. He had shit his diapers as babies do, but my mom felt he was getting too old for this. Since words didn't seem to be working, action was required. I watched as she took his soiled diapers and swung them over her head and then back down across his little body. "Don't you ever, ever do that again," she screamed. Her own violent toilet training at the hands of her mother—had taken over. I was witnessing a full-blown episode of post-traumatic stress disorder. (That diagnosis wouldn't be listed in the DSM for another twenty years.) I quietly sidled out of the room as she continued to flog and scream at my baby brother.

After that, poop was loaded, an endless source of fascination. I began to covertly experiment with shitting in my own underpants. The feeling was exquisite, the warm soft poop melting between my buttocks. The forbidden release, the sensual squishiness of it, was delicious. And then immediately followed by terror. I knew what would happen if my mom found out.

These ecstatic sessions, lasting only a few seconds, would be followed by long minutes in the bathroom scrubbing and scrubbing. My mother could never know.

One day found me in the basement of the house, in a wood paneled room furnished with large red leather chairs studded with gleaming brass upholstery nails. A mahogany bar lined one side of the room Opening a hidden panel in one of the walls, I slipped into the unfinished corridor behind it. I can still see the long narrow hallway stretching before me, the concrete under my feet, pipes above.

All of a sudden the urge was upon me and I was undoing my pants, pulling them down, squatting, shitting on the bare floor. I was just relaxing into the delicious sense of release when I saw the shadow. My mother.

She was wordless at first, just grabbed my forearms, forced my hands down into the small warm pile, and then started rubbing them over my face. She found her voice after that and began to scream. "You filthy, disgusting little animal. You filthy disgusting animal!" Completely possessed, she screamed these words over and over as she frog marched me out of the basement, up the stairs, into the bathroom.

She held me in front of the mirror, forced me to stare at my reflection, continued to berate me. My face had been disfigured as if by some terrible disease. My smooth pink cheeks, nose, forehead were covered by a brown, pudding-like surface, all ridges and valleys. I no longer appeared human. My mom abruptly stopped screaming, dropped my hands, and left me alone in the bathroom, continuing to gaze at myself.

And now, in Ireland, in 2008, Michael was asking us to look in a mirror as we sobbed, report back. But this time I was in a room filled with loving adults. We all knew trauma, had worked on it for many years, and were all aware what a unique opportunity this was to be able to reveal our wounded child amidst such a concentration of love and compassion. Again and again, I was privileged to witness the deepest secret pain of another and to have my own agony witnessed and held in turn. I had never before been in a room so filled with tears and with laughter, so much anguish and such joy.

135

As we neared the end of the week, Michael held up a print of Edward Munch's "The Scream." I have never been able to bear looking at this painting, its uncontained agony, but Michael spoke of how Munch had captured one of the essential truths of being human— that moment of unbearable suffering, that moment when we could no longer contain our pain. The breaking point. Our mission, he said, was to recall all the "Scream moments" in our lives, starting with the first one we could remember, and then share them, one by one, in our triads. We would each have the opportunity, in turn, to share, to witness, and finally to hold the position of the person who had caused such suffering.

Because my experience of screaming in the forest was so recent, when my turn came, I chose to begin with that and work my way backward instead. In terrible detail, I made my way through my life, again and again recalling moments where I had reached the breaking point. Starting with the agony I had felt about losing Tracey, I worked my way back through the decades, finally reaching that terrible day in front of the mirror in Kentucky. And even before that, alone in the crib. But how about before that?

Here I had to rely on a combination of gut feeling and stories I had been told. Because, I was the first child, everything in my early development was completely new and uncertain for my mother. She lacked the confidence of a veteran parent that children will learn, eventually, to wean themselves, sleep through the night, not shit themselves into adulthood. To help herself get through this uncertainty, she made a volume of copious notes on my every move during my first years. She bequeathed this book to me when I was eighteen and I used it extensively in therapy to help recall my early childhood.

One remarkable thing my mother had done was to nurse me at her breast. I am one of a very small cohort of upper middle class white American men born in the 1950's to have been breastfed. At a time when nursing was medically "contra-indicated" as primitive and

136

unsanitary, my mother had been inspired by some radical thinkers at the time to give breastfeeding a try.

However, this was at a time when very little knowledge existed about how to proceed. There was no La Leche League, no supportive midwives, no shelf of books in the bookstore. So while my mom was able to get through the challenging first days of nursing, when her milk supply diminished after twelve weeks, she gave up. Very abruptly and without warning, when I was twelve weeks old, the breast was taken away and replaced by formula in a bottle. (WHO recommends mothers breastfeed for at least two years.) It's a date my mother duly noted and which I continue to mark on my calendar: July 4. My mother wrote how reluctant I had been to make the switch, how she had to put sugar on the rubber nipple to get me to go along.

So now, sitting in this workshop in Ireland, looking out the window across the water at the craggy form of Skellig Michael, the jagged rocks of that ancient monastic retreat wavering in the mist, my partners asked me if there was an earlier Scream I could remember. There was. The day the breast did not come. I couldn't remember it in my mind. I had only my mother's words for that. But the feeling of that abrupt absence—the bottomless gnawing hunger that nothing ever managed to fill, not food, not alcohol, not pot, not sex. I could remember that feeling.

When I was a teenager, my grandmother would sometimes ask me to close my mouth. In repose, I left it hanging open, as I had all through childhood, and she feared I would never stop. "I can't bear it," she would say. "It's the same expression you had on your face when you would crawl after your mother, moaning, when you were just a few months' old." I may have learned to close my mouth as an adult, but the longing never left.

"Time's up," Michael announced. "Switch roles."

On the wall above me, an ancient Tibetan lama, only days away from death, gazed down at me out of a framed photograph. He stared at me with urgency. He seemed to know exactly what was going on. And, as a matter of fact, I knew a little about him, too.

His name was Jamyang Khyentse Chokyi Lodro, and he had been the beloved mentor and inspiration for Sogyal Rinpoche, author of the spiritual classic, The Tibetan Book of Living and Dying.   Sogyal Rinpoche's organization, Rigpa, was the owner of this retreat center and pictures of Jamyang Khyentse were everywhere.   He had been the teacher of many of the greatest Tibetan teachers who came to America and was a master of the rites and initiations of all four major schools of Tibetan Buddhism.   And he had been showing up in my life for the past two years.

It started when I was introduced to *The Tibetan Book of Living and Dying* in 2006 along with some books by E.Evans-Wentz, one of the first to introduce Tibetan Buddhism to the West.   E. Evans-Wentz kept referring to Manjushri, the boddhisatva of wisdom, and I was fascinated by this figure who was portrayed in thankas as half man and half woman, carrying a flaming sword in his right hand and the Heart Sutra in his left. I resonated deeply with this depiction of wisdom as both the sword which cuts through all illusion and the lotus text which gently conveys enlightenment.   His combination of yin and yang, of violence and sweetness, captured the essence of what, to me, wisdom truly is, truly requires.

I realized I needed a thanka of my own and went on eBay.   I immediately found a beautiful silk painting of this embodiment of wisdom with the i.d. code, EM4U. My name at the time was still Emery, an old family name from my mother's side which had gone back and forth between men and women over the previous four generations. My friends called me Em for short. EM4U. Em, for you.

I won the bid and received the painting.   It was a unique "initatory" thanka, the seller told me and certainly this particular portrayal was distinct: the figure of the bodhisattva was the traditional androgyne bearing flaming sword and text resting on a lotus, but the background was jet black, sprinkled with stars. It looked as if Manjushri were travelling through space in a translucent sphere.

On the day the thanka arrived, I leafed through *The Tibetan Book of Living and Dying* to see if it contained any references to this unusual boddhisattva. I learned that Jamyang Khyentse, the lama looking down at me from the wall in Ireland, had always been strongly associated with Manjushri. Some believed he was actually his incarnation.

And now, this incarnation of a bodhisattva with a flaming sword and a book of wisdom was hearing my first scream and indicating that I should pay close attention. Michael Murphy had interrupted me just as I had been about to share this original "Scream" with my partners. I couldn't tell them about it; it was time to move on. My turn was over. But something in Jamyang Khyentse's eyes as he stared benevolently yet urgently down at me told me that he heard and that I must pay attention.

Michael's workshop had no affiliation with Rigpa, but the retreat center's hosts offered us meditation every morning and the next morning, as usual, I joined the pre-breakfast sit. On the altar were thankas of the Buddha and also a photo of the omnipresent Jamyang Khyentse. He was a friendlier here, more relaxed.

I knew something of the circumstances of his death, in June 1959, two months after I was born. He had made it out of Tibet before the Chinese seized the entire country and took refuge in neighboring Sikkim. Hundreds of exiled monks and other lamas, in turn, took refuge at his feet. Surely this great lama, living bodhisattva, would know what to do. But Jamyang Khyentse was dying. As the great monasteries and monastic colleges of Tibet were destroyed one by one by the Chinese army, he grew weaker and weaker, as if he were being killed blow by blow. And some of the pictures around the retreat center revealed the great lama's anguish, his despair.

So, sitting on my cushion, I felt into this man's final "Scream" and, at the same time, felt into my own first one, which had occurred just a few days later in real time. Jamyang Khyentse died on June 28, 1959. And I knew, from the notes my mother so carefully made, that I had been weaned six days later. I imagined his desperation and felt into my own as the beloved breast was taken away much too soon. Abandonment, desolation, hopelessness, rage—we were each—man and infant—racked by the same terrible feelings, the anguish which accompanied the lama as he left this world and, just days later, was with me as I more fully entered it. Although one trauma was global in its repercussions, the other tiny and personal, they shared a core betrayal and desolation.

At that moment, the fire alarm went off and the meditation room was filled with an electric screaming and flashing. I worked hard to maintain my focus. There was no smoke, no sign of fire. Stay present, my inner voice admonished. And then, just as abruptly, the screaming stopped. The alarm went off and the lights returned to normal. I continued to feel into the overwhelming anguish, but it wasn't anguish anymore. The inner scream had stopped, too.

In its place was the most exquisite sensation of peace, of everything being not only all right, but better than you could ever have imagined. My cushion felt like it was floating above the carpet. My consciousness had lifted out of the realm of impermanence and suffering into a heaven of the deepest joy, the deepest peace.

I realized, too, that I had been here before: on the third day of my vision quest twelve years earlier, when the transcendent Beeeeeeeeeeeeeee! had lifted me up, carried me for hours. What was this? It was way better than any drug I had ever taken, more ecstatic than my most extraordinary sexual experience, beyond even holding my children when they were first born. And it went on and on. I floated through the rest of the day.

And, as it had twelve years ago in the woods, the feeling slowly faded as I gently sank back down into normal awareness. And, just as I had years

140

before, I knew I had touched on something that was more important than anything else. And Jamyang Khyentse seemed to agree. As I walked down the hall out of the central meeting room, I saw a picture of him I had not noticed before. Here, he was beaming and his hand was in the universal mudra, hand position, of A-OK: thumb and forefinger in a circle, the other three fingers upright exclamation points. In Buddhism, this hand gesture is called the "Vitarka Mudra" and it evokes the wordless transmission of enlightenment.

It would be another year before I received a reasonable explanation of what had happened. Eckhart Tolle spelled it out in *A New Earth*, his follow up to *The Power of Now*. That Power? It is the extraordinary feeling of joy that underlies all experience, usually obscured by endless thinking. It is the joy of simply being, of simply existing. And, according to Tolle, the ancient Indians had a word for it: *ananda.*

I had been leading vision quests for nine years. I learned from the dozens of questers I worked with, each with his or her own burning question, there were really only two questions: "Who am I?"and "What is my purpose?" And, if you answered one of them, you had the answer to both. They were two sides of the same coin.

So now, even though my original vision question in 1996 had been "what is my purpose?," in that moment reading Eckhart Tolle explaining ananda, I knew who I was. If my purpose was to be, then I was the other side of the coin: this overwhelming feeling of joy, ananda. I had finally answered Sai Baba's question from nine years before—Who are you?

On these two occasions—in the New York woods in August of 1996 and on the Irish coast in May of 2008—— I had been shown who I really was. I remembered my grade school coach's words, quoting the Patriots' receivers coach: If you can touch it, you can catch it.

I had touched IT. Twice. Now I was determined to catch it.

Chapter 11

Death

After my grandmother, Sue, my favorite family member was Joanna. My first memory of her was something she gave me: the best christening gifts I received at age six—an illustrated edition of stories about the knights of the Round Table and a big box of maple sugar candy. She was my godmother as well as my aunt and took her duties seriously. Fifteen years before I knew I wanted to be an Indian, she had married a real one, my Uncle Ellis.

He wrote a blessing at the time of my birth, wishing for me a lifelong appreciation of irony. And this has been the secret of my survival. Enjoying, or at least welcoming, the fact that things are often the opposite of what you expect is powerful wisdom. The concept of fierce grace was a perfect example of such dancing with irony, and its liberative impact was in many ways the fruit of Ellis's blessing all those years before. But, like Ellis, Joanna was a lifelong smoker. The habit killed him before he reached seventy and although she came from a family where people typically lived well into their eighties, she received the diagnosis of Stage Four lung cancer in the spring of 2009. She was 76.

By December, it was evident Joanna had only had a few weeks left and she was very clear. She did not want flowers or any kind of fancy funeral. She wanted donations sent to the Hopital Albert Schweitzer in Haiti. Her specificity was puzzling. But her generosity was not. Even though she was an upper class WASP by birth, she identified strongly with the downtrodden. In 1965, she went to Mississippi to help register African-American voters. She helped rat-proof tenements in Michigan slums in the late 1960's. She worked (until cancer prevented her) the night shift at a local nursing home, changing bedpans and providing comfort to elderly people largely abandoned by their own families. She had always given money to the Poor Clares, a sister organization to the Franciscans. It made sense that her last wish would be to send money to some of the most desperate people on Earth.

By mid January, Joanna was on her deathbed. After listening to her rattling breath, her brother, Henry, an internist with decades of experience caring for the elderly, said she had seventy-two hours left. We agreed I would sit with her the first night. None of us—my brothers, my dad, my uncle—wanted her to be alone at the end. We would all take shifts at her bedside.

Joanna never had children and made no secret that babies made her nervous. "I am happy to be with children who can read," she would say, "Because then, if things become awkward, we can always play library." This game involved everyone in the room reading quietly to themselves, an activity I have found handy with my own children. When I arrived at her bedside that final evening, Joanna showed no interest in any kind of "final" conversation. She suggested I peruse one of the New Yorkers on her bedside table while she simply laid her hand on the mystery novel she had been reading. She no longer had energy to actually pick the book up, but she was determined we play a final round of library.

143

A little while later, she started to ask me something, but noticed I was engrossed in Talk of the Town. "Oh, but you're reading."

Those were her last words.

A few moments later, she went into respiratory arrest and I ran from the room to get a nurse. They gave her oxygen and a morphine drip while the doctor showed me her most recent x-rays. "Here are her lungs a week ago," he showed me her right lung, half white with the toxic fluid it contained. "And here is the x-ray from this afternoon." The same lung was now entirely white. "All we can do now is try and make her as comfortable as possible."

She had asked that her brother, Henry, be by her bedside at the end. I went to the nearby motel where he was staying and banged on his door. He appeared in his underwear, hair disheveled.

"It's time."

It was a little after one AM and Henry and I spent Joanna's final hours chatting beside the bed as she, now in a morphine-induced coma, struggled for breath. It reminded me of the birth of my children, but in reverse. We were in that same outside-of-time place, where all one's ordinary obligations were suspended, but instead of measuring the intervals between contractions as they shortened in anticipation of my child's entrance into the world, here we sat listening to the gaps grow between Joanna's tortured breaths. Eventually, instead of an infant bawling, there would be silence.

Henry recalled the last words of his mother, my Grandmother, Sue. "It was maybe twenty-four hours before she died and the nurse had just asked her if she would like some more morphine. And what do you think she said?" He was chuckling. "'Why, yes. That would be delightful.'" He imitated the way Sue would tip her head and smile up at whoever was serving her, the way she would lift her hand in a gentle

144

sweep of encouragement. He was beaming. "Just as if she were at a tea party and had been offered another cup."

We both smiled at this memory of Sue's graciousness, her capacity for joy. I was allowing myself to sink into the memory when Henry touched my arm. "I think she's gone." And, just like that, Joanna was no longer with us, as if her spirit had ridden her brother's hand up into the air as he gestured in remembered joy, "Why, yes! That would be delightful." And even though she was dead, the air was thick with a charged energy, just as it was at the birth of my children. And, just as then, I felt I had received an extraordinary blessing, the privilege of being with this beloved woman as she took her final breath.

The next day, Haiti was struck by a devastating earthquake.

A couple of months later, I went on my second silent meditation retreat. Nine days, no talking. For someone as voluble as me, this would be like a month of silence for a normal person My good friend, Bill, the same man who had given me *Ram Dass: Fierce Grace*, had recommended the experience to me. He knew how impactful my vision quest experiences had been. "I think you may find this even more powerful."

He sent me to the Insight Meditation Society, IMS, whose headquarters were a former Catholic monastery in central Massachusetts. They had a single bowling lane where the Dalai Lama had once bowled. Now, it was used for walking meditation.

A good friend said she loved these retreats except that, for the first two days, she felt like she was trapped in a telephone booth with a crazy person. And it was true. During the first days of silence, my ego went into overdrive, trying to make up for the absence of talking, trying to make sure I remembered how important it was.

The breaking point came during the morning of the second day when I had just about convinced myself that silence wasn't for me and what I really needed was an Egg McMuffin. I was on the verge of rising from my meditation cushion, heading to my truck, when the sheer craziness of my thinking stopped me. That I had almost been able to convince myself of the absolute necessity of something so banal shocked my mind into silence. And that silence, that instant of mental quiet, was much more delicious than food.

The IMS protocol was very traditional, cleaving as closely as possible to the original regime at the Buddha's first monastery. So while we did not have to go out and beg for our food, we did arise at five a.m. and meditate continuously until ten p.m., alternating between sitting and walking sessions all day. We were given two vegetarian meals, which all fifty of us ate together in silence—perhaps the hardest part of the day for me. Sitting, surrounded by people you cannot speak with or make eye contact with, while eating, went against all my training. If you sit with people while you eat, you make conversation. This is how normal humans behave. And, while Buddha's monks ate nothing after the midday meal, we were given a light supper of soup each afternoon.

Our sitting meditation was supposed to take place in the meditation hall, a large open room filled with dozens of rows of cushions, chairs around the edge for people whose knees couldn't take it anymore. Many people prefer to meditate in groups. They say it helps them focus, increases the power of the experience. For me, it was distracting. In the Buddha's day, men and women sat separately and I wished that were the case here. No matter how hard I tried not to, I would always locate the three or four most attractive women in the hall and then one would fix in my mind.

When I embarrassedly told my friend, Bill, about this after my first retreat, he laughed. "Ah, the IMS 'romance.'" He reminded me that that was the first test Buddha faced under the Bodhi Tree. "Everyone goes through that. Then comes fear." He paused. "And, last of all, doubt."

I took a short cut. I would do the first few sessions in the hall and then seek a less distracting location elsewhere. I found a quiet study upstairs.

To concentrate my mind, I started to practice Metta—sending lovingkindness to everyone at the retreat. I placed my hand over my heart center, deepened my in-breath, my out-breath, and pictured the glow in my chest radiating out toward all the other people in the meditation hall. After a while, I expanded my attention to include everyone who had ever attended a retreat here. The sheer magnitude of the numbers, the years, quieted my mind.

Some time later, my attention returned to the room. As I surveyed the furniture, the lamps, a small statue of the Buddha, my eyes came to the coffee table in the middle of the room. At the center of the table was a photograph of an elderly Indian woman, all in white. She looked almost impossibly small and reminded me physically of how my Aunt Joanna had appeared during her final days in the hospital—a little girl, encased in what looked like white gauze, but surrounded by a huge aura of power, much too large to fit in such a tiny body. At the center of this tableau were her eyes, huge and brown and deeply kind. I could not look away.

I heard her speaking in my mind. "What a thoughtful young man. I will give you a transmission." First my body and then the entire room began to fill with a warm, white, pulsating light. The feeling was blissful and seemed to go on and on. After a while, the feeling subsided and I was sitting alone in the room again, but the picture on the coffee table still held a kernel of light. The old woman appeared to be smiling at me.

I did not learn until after the retreat that this woman was called Dipa Ma, "Mother of Light," and that she had been a sort of guru for the founders of IMS. She lived in a two-room apartment with her daughter, Dipa, in a poor neighborhood in Calcutta, where she dispensed tea and wisom, her devotees learning of her through word of mouth. She never taught publicly, never wrote anything, but somehow developed a wide following, including young Americans. Some of these Americans had been at the same meditation retreats attended by Ram Dass and his followers. Some of these young Americans went on to find Maharaj-ji. Others found Dipa Ma.

Although the initial transmission from Dipa Ma was powerful, it did not prepare me for what was to come. The final morning of the retreat, I was sitting in the dining hall, drinking tea, and a clarity came over me. If my longing, any kind of longing, were outwardly directed, if I believed that my longing needed to be satisfied by something outside myself, I was still at the level of a nursing baby. I had yet to be weaned. Only when I realized that longing could only be satisfied from within, by who I already was, would I be free.

This truth came not only as words but as an oceanic knowing, a feeling which swept through me. It was that simple. If I could remember to turn to my heart for succor, all would be well. The simplicity of this truth staggered me. Did I look within or did I seek outside? One choice set me free. The other was bondage.

The lightness I felt was extraordinary. I flowed out of the cafeteria and into the meditation hall. I was free. It had been that easy. There really was nothing—no thing—to it.

As the retreat leader gave his final talk, I floated over my cushion. The work was done. I had made it. Enlightenment had come at last. All that stuff written in so many books over so many years by so many people? It was all right here. Now. Every second of every day.

And then, after the talk was over and the rule of silence lifted, I made the mistake of opening my mouth. As soon as I said something to the woman sitting next to me, and she responded with a slight difference of opinion, I was back in duality. Just how Peter must have felt when the wind picked up after he had gotten out of the boat to follow Jesus, had actually been inspired to take two steps on water. The panic that came over him, the overwhelming doubt that made his knees buckle, his feet lose their purchase, and put him once again back in rough water. I was back in the world of clashing egos where some were right, others wrong, and I was trapped in the endless chop of changing appearances and preferences. I couldn't even hear Jesus's words to Peter when he lost his nerve. "Ye of little faith."

I could, however, hear my friend, Bill. "And, last of all, doubt." This was the final hurdle. It wasn't just about touching the ball and catching it. It was about being able to hold on to this knowing and walk with it out into the world.

Dipa Ma's advice to everyone who came before her was the same: Meditate more. And by more, she didn't mean to try to up your sit from twenty to thirty minutes. She meant to increase your daily meditation from two hours to four or six or, better yet, eight hours every day. She meant give your life to meditation. Only by this would you be free. It might sound extreme, but I had tasted that freedom. I had been enlightened for forty-five minutes. There was no going back.

When I explained to Tracey, after I got home, that I would now be doing a two hour sit every morning and every evening, and a midday sit whenever possible, she wasn't surprised. In some ways, it wasn't all that different from where Maharaj-ji's marching orders were taking her, more and more deeply into vinyasa yoga and kirtan. More and more out into the world. She was reinventing herself as a committed musician and yogini. And I was becoming an increasingly committed yogi, disappearing into study and meditation for hours every day. Going more and more within. We had had less and less to talk about for months. Our separation was well under way.

However, while I happily believed I was on the fast track to liberation, I had no idea how deep my attachment to Tracey actually ran. That awakening would come at the end of the summer, when Drex came to visit.

My first memory of Drex was his big smile, long brown hair swinging, as he bounded up the driveway to meet me, right hand outstretched for a hearty shake. Tracey and I ran summer camps for kids and Drex came highly recommended as a counselor. A little younger than me, with boundless enthusiasm and a lot of experience, he was an obvious choice. The fact he had a great set of abs and never wore a shirt didn't seem to pose a problem.

During the first weeks of camp, he and I became fast friends. Drex was also becoming close to Tracey, but because she and I had drifted so far apart, this was not on my radar.

Probably the first obvious clue, besides his never wearing a shirt, was a story he told about being in a bar once and a woman asking him where he got the name, Drex. "Oh," he said, "My mom was a hippy, big into sex, drugs and rock 'n' roll, so she named me after her two favorite things." He laughed when I asked if the line had been successful.

Even two months after camp was over, I did not suspect anything when he came to visit, saying he was on fire with enthusiasm for life after working with Tracey and me. "Just Spirit Hollow working its magic," I thought to myself. I was a little surprised when Tracey burst in while I was meditating, a day or two after he arrived. "We have to talk."

She rushed out of the room to get Drex. A moment later, I was sitting between them on the couch. I could now begin to feel something a little strange, an unfamiliar tension. Why was the air so thick?

"We have to tell you," Tracey said. "There are feelings between Drex and me that we have to explore."

Everything began to move very slowly and in complete silence. I was across the room, watching the three of us sitting on the couch that had been a wedding present from my father. Tracey was putting a gun to the side of my head, pulling the trigger. There was no sound, no blood. There was no pain. But it was over.

150

And then I was back on the couch, sitting between them, feeling like a parent who had just caught his daughter climbing out her bedroom window, trying to elope. These crazy kids! All I could feel was relief that this wasn't happening to me. They were both married to other people, had kids. Thank God I wasn't in their situation.

Just like when I broke my arm skiing in high school, it took a while for the dissociated thoughts to subside, for the pain of what had just happened to begin to register.

I made no connection between my decision to essentially leave my wife in order to meditate and this outrage. In the days that followed, even though I was still going through the motions of my new meditation practice, what was happening on the cushion could in no way be termed "meditation." All I could do was run endless mental tape of my wife with another man. Nor could I even remotely appreciate how my kissing Kiera a few years before could have in any way led to my current circumstances. Tracey's behavior was inexcusable, and that's all there was to it. I asked her to go into therapy and sat down to wait for her to return to her senses.

This didn't happen. When Tracey's therapist asked her to look into the reasons she had fallen in love with another man, she confirmed what I had already been figuring out over the past few years: we had grown apart to where we no longer enjoyed each other's company. Sure, we had once been the "shaman twins." And it had been an amazing synchronicity that we had both felt called by Maharaj-ji. However, neither of us ever stopped to examine the consequences of being "lucky" enough to meet one's guru.

The divergent paths the guru sent us on—meditation and increasing introversion for me—performing and teaching and increasing extroversion for her—meant that it was only a matter of time before the two of us were out of radio contact. What was most important to me was boring to Tracey. What lit her up looked like vanity to me. We

151

rarely talked except about logistics. Our only real intimacy was our once-a-week love making which I secretly thought of as my "last addiction." However, no matter how much Tracey's falling for Drex made "sense," it brought up all my submerged attachment and infantile needs. All I knew was that I had been betrayed and abandoned and it was Tracey's fault.

I had trouble sleeping for the first time in my life. When I woke up to pee, my mind would fill with thoughts, images, outrage, about Tracey and Drex. Endless mental tape would loop and I would toss and turn for hours.

I forbade Tracey to see Drex. She was married, had children, I observed righteously. She had a commitment. She stopped sleeping with me. I lasted about seven weeks before it occurred to me that she was an adult and could see whomever she chose. However, by that time, Drex and his wife had made up and recommitted themselves. Tracey and I couldn't do the same.

I knew from my retreat in Ireland that my first "scream" was my abrupt weaning at three months. So, when my brother was born three years later and I was sent away to preschool while he got to stay at home and nurse—that would have been another scream.

This was a conscious memory. My mother, little brother in her arms, was walking me up the path to the preschool door one morning, saying goodbye as I went inside, and something snapped. I couldn't take it anymore. As my mother turned and went back down the path on her way home, I ran after her, screaming. "Take me home, too!" But before I reached her, another quieter voice in my head said, "You know, this is never going to work. No way is she taking you home." And before I even reached my mom, as she was just starting to turn around, my tears had stopped and I was heading back to school. And that was my first experience of "the witness," the wise quiet voice of the Self that is always with us, who sees with complete dispassion how it is, guiding us from within, if we can quiet our thoughts enough to listen.

I can still remember the first day I went to work in New York City, early on in my relationship with Nancy. We walked to work together for a few blocks, but then I had to take the subway to Manhattan for my summer job at a law firm. She kept walking; the school she taught at was right there in Brooklyn. The longing I felt as I descended the steps into the tunnel took me right back to that moment at preschool. One reason I would choose to teach alongside Nancy after law school is that I didn't want to feel that empty feeling.

And once again, with Tracey, I had created a world where we could teach together in the same place, at least a lot of the time. Once again, my life had been carefully constructed so as to never have to feel that abandonment

I was now confronted with the feeling beneath that feeling of being sent away—the awareness that the woman I loved most in the world no longer loved me in the same way. I was trapped in an endless loop of running down that preschool path and knowing, at the same time, that it was never going to work.

I walked a lot during this time. It was the only way I could get relief. There was a huge oak in the woods where I would go and it became a trusted friend. Just as I had embraced trees for comfort when I was two, I embraced this oak every time I reached him. Something about grasping his rough bark, pressing my whole body against his solid, unyielding trunk, soothed me. I would look up at the rustling leaves, brown and dead yet unable to let go, and sink into their endless murmuring.

One day, I was embracing my friend and something was different. I looked up and the leaves were gone, carried off by the November winds. Instead of its murmuring whisper, the oak was silent. And my mind quieted for a moment. The leaves had been my thoughts, endlessly whispering, telling the sad story of my life over and over and over. But now they were gone. The story had stopped.

Yes, it was awful how Tracey had hurt me. Yes it was awful that the marriage was over. But, much more awful than either of these truths, were the cruel stories my mind insisted on telling me again and again, how I had been abandoned and betrayed, abandoned and betrayed….

How about if I just stopped telling the stories?

I felt the oak speaking in my mind:

When you stand at the threshold of liberation, why would you choose to run back into bondage?

Chapter 12

The Joy of Powerlessness

Soon afterward, Tracey and I got down to the business of separating. She would stay at Spirit Hollow with the kids and I would move to a spiritually-oriented nature preserve called Manitou on the other side of the state, taking the job of Events Director. Maia and Noah would stay with me on weekends. Tracey would buy me out after the kids were grown and, in the meantime, she would run Spirit Hollow without me.

Manitou had first come on my radar three years earlier, right after I met Amma, when Tracey and I were hitting the wall for the first time. Tracey was in the middle of running a women's workshop and I was watching the kids when I spotted a woman I didn't know walking up the driveway. Her head was haloed with snow white hair and her blue eyes sparkled. Her name was Sylvia Blanchet and she had come from Manitou to see how a "similarly situated" spiritual center made ends meet.

Our two organizations had a lot in common. Both centered on large parcels of undeveloped Vermont forest. Both had been started by passionate individuals (Pam Meyer, in the case of Manitou) who first purchased the land themselves and then inspired a circle of friends to gather around them to mindfully develop the land in order to create spiritual programs. Manitou's supporters had created an extensive trail network on their land, something we had hoped to do, and we had created two workshop-ready structures—insulated yurts with wood stoves—and were offering a regular program of workshops to ensure a steady income stream, something which Manitou aspired to.

Sylvie and I chatted for a while and she invited me to visit Manitou, outside Brattleboro, just forty miles away in the southeastern corner of the state. That began an informal cooperation between our sister organizations. Over the next three years, I would teach a shamanic workshop for them and Pam's son, Mike became a good friend. When it came time for me to leave Spirit Hollow, I knew where I wanted to go.

Mike was enthusiastic about the idea. He needed someone to help design and administer programming at Manitou as well as assistance stewarding the land. I was the perfect jack-of-all-trades for the job.

In October of 2011, I took down one of our yurts and loaded it into a truck. By the end of the next month, it was set up at Manitou — 250 wooded acres in the mountains outside Brattleboro—and I had moved in. No electricity, no running water. My light came from oil lamps and my water would be drawn from a nearby stream. I built a composting toilet and Mike said I could shower at his house once or twice a week. My new life as a hermit, something I had always loved the idea of, had begun. Maia and Noah weren't crazy about the lifestyle, but they went along graciously.

At first, I ran amok. Freed from the restraints of monogamy, a parent only on weekends. I didn't want to break up anybody's marriage. I knew what that felt like. But any single woman from twenty to fifty was a prospect. I was a kid in a candy store.

I also started smoking cigarettes again and smoking pot on a regular basis. And it could all be justified. Sex was tantric. Tobacco was sacred.

And marijuana was a shamanic "teaching plant." I had the textual references to prove it. Never mind that my underlying driver was the grief of being ripped from my life of living with Tracey and Maia and Noah. And the older abandonment this grief triggered.

I became, as a wise sober friend later observed, "skinny and manic." This period lasted about nine months before I found I couldn't outrun my grief. I woke up one morning completely empty. What was happening to me? I had been a husband, a father, a respected spiritual teacher, and now I was turning into a stoner horn dog who was getting shut down a lot more than he was getting lucky. I couldn't pay my bills.

I was in my fifties and had nothing to show for it. Everything I had worked so hard for—marriage, children, house and land, spiritual center, community, the contacts I needed to find carpentry work— gone. Maybe I should just finish the job. My mind went to "strategy number two": suicide. Just turn up the dial on acting out. If sex and drugs won't do it, pull the plug. The ultimate tantrum.

Fortunately, twelve-step wisdom kicked in. This was just my brain on drugs. I didn't need to kill myself. I needed a meeting. The next day found me at the "Nooner," the daily twelve p.m. meeting at the Baptist church in town. I raised my hand, busted myself. I told the group what had happened to my sobriety. It was embarrassing, but I was home.

The best thing I heard that day was from an old-timer: "the joy of powerlessness." The irony of this statement grabbed me. I had a new koan to work with.

It wasn't long before this riddle was put to the test. I was in the woods, clearing a view at Manitou, impatiently chainsawing, two words which should never be in the same sentence. I had brought down a large oak and it had fallen on numerous saplings which, bent over by the large tree's weight, had the effrontery to be in my way.

It all happened very slowly. The sapling, maybe the thickness of a broomstick, was bent over like a big upside down U, its leafy end trapped beneath the fallen oak. I ran the blade through the little maple close to where it disappeared and instantly felt my mistake. As if in slow motion, the severed end of the sapling hovered in the air, sampling its freedom, before beginning its return skyward. I watched in horrified fascination as the shaft of wood moved toward my face with increasing speed, like a bat swung for the fences.

"This is really going to hurt," it occurred to me right before I was punched in the face, much harder than I had ever been hit before. Then I was on all fours, spitting blood. "Wow," I thought with the detachment peculiar to serious injury, "This would make a great poster for the First Step." Came to realize we were powerless and our lives had become unmanageable.

Lying on a bed in the emergency room, concealed behind curtains, listening to a faceless man groaning a couple of feet away, awaiting the verdict on my injury, it occurred to me that I did not have health insurance. In my stoned bliss of the previous months, I had put all the renewal notices in a pile on the floor, waiting for "later." I wondered how much all this was going to cost.

And, as I lay there for hours, contemplating my fate, I wondered if this was what dying felt like. The throbbing in my jaw went in and out of sync with the second hand of the clock on the wall. Control over every aspect of my life had slipped through my fingers. Who was I? What was I? How would I pay for my careless accident, much less my food, for the next six months?

When the ER doc finally reached me, she told me that nothing was broken. I would just need nine stitches under my chin. However, the bill, which arrived a couple of weeks later, was another thing— $5200. That's a lot of money when you don't have any. One Ben Franklin for each year of my life. Fortunately, I was making so little that I was covered by the hospital's generous assistance program for the uninsured.

In addition to being Manitou's groundskeeper, I was "Events Coordinator," responsible for designing programming, scheduling events, and doing publicity. Even though I had little interest in this— publicity had been Tracey's department at Spirit Hollow— my association with her success had gotten me this gig. How long it would last was anybody's guess.

One day, talking with Mike and Fred, another Manitou board member, about getting the word out, Facebook came up. We knew it was essential to modern publicity, but, as three middle-aged men in 2012, we knew nothing more. We needed someone who did.

Both Mike and Fred came up with the answer at the same time: iishana! Apparently iishana Artra, another Manitou supporter, was savvy about social media. They were sure she would be happy to give me a lesson. And so began a leisurely game of telephone tag where iishana and I took turns leaving each other messages, suggesting times which never seemed to work for the other. Finally, several months later, at the end of May, we found a time and my first Facebook lesson was on the calendar.

I had been warned. Mike knew a little about iishana, having tried unsuccessfully to date her, and told me to be wary. Iishana might know about social media, but she was "narcissistic" and had a tendency "to use men." I wasn't too worried. After a year of striking out repeatedly in a stoned haze, I was ready to give the ladies a rest.

When iishana opened her front door, she glowed. A golden light appeared to encircle her head and her deep brown eyes shone. Her teeth flashed in a smile as she welcomed me into her home.

We sat in front of the computer screen and immediately lost ourselves in conversation. She had recently completed a master's on life purpose and that was about the only thing on my mind. As we went back and forth about what was most important in life, how you could know you had found your true calling, we settled back in our chairs, looking straight ahead. The conversation had gone deep. Our eyes were closed now and the pauses were getting longer.

I shared my core insight from leading vision quests for ten years: our deepest questions are either "who am I?" —or— "what is my purpose?" And, when you answer one, you will have answered the other.

There was a long pause and then iishana murmured that she largely agreed with me, but that she had found that asking who you were wasn't exactly it, too vague and uncertain The really important question to ask is what am I? Much more solid.

There was a longer pause as I processed this course adjustment. "So what are you?"

After an even longer pause, iishana dreamily answered that she saw, felt, herself as a vast expanse of ocean. I would later learn that this awareness grew from a profound mystical experience she had on Maui, the year before, where she had been meditating on the beach and felt a tsunami-like wave of energy approach her from off shore. She made the conscious choice to surrender to it and, as the immense wave poured over her, through her, she realized she and it were made of the same stuff.

I didn't know any of this yet, but I could see her ocean in my mind's eye, stretching off toward the horizon, its surface vast and flat and so calm. I felt an immense peace. I was standing on the edge of a high cliff looking out over the water and it was clear what I had to do.

I spoke very slowly, as if in a dream, "I have an overwhelming desire to dive into that ocean."

It wasn't a come on. I simply knew that I had just been shown, was feeling very deeply, very clearly, my single purpose in this life.

After the longest pause so far, iishana dreamily intoned, "That would be ideal."

I dove.

In my mind's eye, I plunged headfirst off the cliff's edge. I hit the water and went into bliss. I didn't open my eyes for several minutes. When I finally looked at the computer in front of us, it had gone into screen saver mode. Every few seconds, a different word would slide by. I watched as "indubitable" drifted into view. As it vanished, the screen went blank.

Time moved slowly as, for the next several hours, iishana and I got to know each other, our hopes, our visions, our histories. We never touched that whole day, but the air was thick between us, sweet and tangible, connecting us as intimately as if we had just become lovers.

It turned out she, too, had been longing for a partner who was serious about learning Tantra, not the cliché sexual stuff from the Kama Sutra, but Tantra in the deeper sense where everything is God and the purpose of marriage is to do everything in each other's power to help one another realize this truth. Sex becomes a way of merging with God, as does doing the dishes and taking out the trash. However, iishana and I didn't need any of these activities. We were already there.

Over the next few weeks, iishana and I met several times. In some ways, it was formality. It had been clear by the end of our first encounter that we would be life partners. The rest was details. But we were also ordinary people trying to get to know each other. Could the i's be dotted, the t's crossed?

It felt effortless. After five weeks, iishana's mother, after listening to her daughter's breathless weekly update, observed thoughtfully, "You two aren't two peas in a pod. You are one pea." And that became our code every time we discovered another synchronicity.

But the big test was Amma. Gurus weren't for everybody and I knew it wouldn't work if my next partner wasn't a devotee. I wasn't going to say this, of course. I mean, how would that sound? But I did have some concern.

Another expression we came to adopt was, "See you and raise you." This classic poker challenge captured perfectly how I felt about iishana. Not only did she really see me, not only did she get and appreciate what I truly was, but she raised the bar over and over. If I was interested in Tantra, she had already taken a workshop. If I had been going to see Amma for several years, spending one day a year with Her every year for the previous five years, iishana immediately signed up for the five-day program, held at a convention center in central Massachsetts, and was happy to sleep in her car so as to be able to afford it.

And, while at Amma's program a month and a half after we first met, iishana looked and felt more at home than I did after six years as a devotee. Amma even came to her in a dream and directed her to create a satsang (community of truth seekers) in Brattleboro. Iishana was already well on her way— her name for her home in town was Healing Gate and she had always wanted it to be a spiritual community. Her house and quarter acre yard were the perfect setting for what Amma was asking her to do.

At some point that day, it occurred to me that iishana and I should purchase rings to commemorate our relationship. Not wedding rings, of course; we had only known each other for six weeks. But I felt we needed some physical object to mark this new deepening of our connection. I imagined us each getting a different ring in the big craft market which accompanies Amma's programs, a way to raise money for her charities. However, we came upon a box of identical rings of all different sizes, silver bands inscribed with Amma's mantra, Aum amriteshwaryai namaha (I bow to the joy that is God herself).

162

We went together for our hug and Amma threw rose petals over us and laughed uproariously. What was so funny? We exchanged rings right after. A friend of mine, a longtime Amma devotee, came up to me later. "I saw Amma shower you two with rose petals. That's what she does when she marries people."

We wouldn't be legally married for another two years, but a few months later we did appear before the probate judge. I was changing my name legally for the second time. The first time had been in 2002. Tracey and I had wanted to share a last name, but neither of us wanted to take the other's. We compromised on the middle name we had planned to give our daughter— Forest. Now, in 2012, iishana encouraged me to claim my real name, the one my first vision quest bestowed upon me: Ananda, the bliss of being.

The judge warned me that by undertaking a second name change, I was likely to draw the suspicion of government authorities. While that problem did not occur, my family would balk at being asked to call me by this strange name. It took a while before they would routinely address me as "Ananda." However, iishana's encouragement set me free. My childhood name, my middle name, Emery, had been feeling more and more like a boy's name. It was long past time for me to think of myself as a man

A few months later we went on a trip, using money I made selling old family silver my Aunt Joanna had given me before she died. I would never use it. That lifestyle was in the rear view. It was poignant letting it go, though. It had been my grandparents'—Sue and George—wedding silver. But the woman in the jewelry store was upbeat—"Of course, it's hard letting the past go, but now the energy is freed up for something new. Maybe a trip. Have you ever been to Hawaii?"

Iishana lit up when I told her this. Her time in Maui and it had been life changing. "Oh!" she said, "We have to go! The volcano that created it, Haleakala, is the heart chakra of the planet."

We flew to Maui the following month and spent the two weeks making a slow circumambulation of the central mountain, the classic pilgrimage in many traditions. We quickly left the highly developed west side of Maui and made our way to Hana on the southeast edge where the narrow winding highway along cliffs thins out most of the tourists. We camped out every night, making love in the jungle, sinking more and more deeply into the vibrations of the land.

I have to admit, when iishana said Maui was the "heart chakra" of the planet, I was a little skeptical. How can you know something like that? But, as was often the case with her wildly improbable observations, she was correct. The way I felt walking on the land, especially out in the jungle, away from people, was just like being with Amma, or tuning into Maharaj-ji. My heart melted and I was in bliss. I had never felt this way anywhere else, day after day. Yes, I was totally in love with iishana and yes, Maui is a tropical paradise, but the land felt different than anywhere I had ever been. It was no coincidence that Ram Dass had been living on Maui for the past ten years and would die there six years later.

We finally reached our pilgrimage destination—the summit of Haleakala. Standing at ten thousand feet, gazing over the vast caldera, we were certainly somewhere very special. At the center of the caldera rose a miniature red mountain, very different in color from the surrounding grey-brown landscape. "That's where we will do our ceremony," I said on a hunch. I had never been here before, but I could feel the pull.

On the way down into the caldera we met an astrophysicist and his nephew. The man worked at the observatory there and was taking the morning off. We could see the Big Island to the south, its twin volcanoes, Haleakala's big sisters. Even though it was almost a hundred miles away, it looked close enough to touch. We mentioned this to the astronomer and he agreed. "It is exceptionally clear today. It might even be the clearest day I have ever seen up here." He had been working at the observatory for eleven years.

164

We left the trail and climbed the red slope to our destination. When we reached its summit, we discovered a naturally formed alcove in the stone. Stones had been carefully placed around the opening and an altar arranged inside, pieces of jungle plants, special rocks. Crouching before it, we were permitted to gaze into the heart center of the island itself, this tender and vulnerable opening at the center of a vast and barren Mars-scape.

I created a second altar with objects I had brought from the mainland— a large crystal, a statue of Hanuman, flowers and chocolates and fruit from below. And here beneath an immense azure dome at the center of the biggest body of water on Earth, ten thousand feet up into the clearest sky the local astronomer had ever seen, iishana and I made our marriage vows—to have an "earth wedding" in the near future, to follow this tantric path wherever it led us, prayers of gratitude that we had somehow been blessed to find each other, two tiny beings in this impossibly large world.

It was hard to go back to Vermont in January. I had left my job at Manitou and moved my yurt to iishana's back yard where we were living in it. I had created small curtain-lined areas— like on a train sleeper car— for my kids to sleep in on weekends. Maia was nine now and Noah was six. They got along ok with iishana and we would play board games on the couch when they came.

But Vermont winters are cold and dark and I only had one adjunct class to teach at the local community college— Introduction to Cultural Anthropology. A depression settled over me that I would struggle with for the next two years. I loved iishana, but, as the old saw has it, "Wherever you go, there you are." Or as Jim from my former men's group put it, "Whenever you follow your bliss, you will come up against all the fears which kept you from your bliss before." Before I could go any further, I was going to have to deal with some of those fears.

Chapter 13

Cruisifixion (sic)

I could barely support myself for the next couple of years, never being offered enough adjunct teaching positions to make my nut and lacking the connections needed to find steady carpentry jobs to cover any shortfalls. I relied heavily on credit cards until I defaulted on them in late 2013. This was my financial bottom and I knew it. Two months later, iishana went through a serious health crisis. I supported her during it, but I was mired in depression. Germinating the heart seed sometimes requires periods of darkness and inaction. Cracking open, putting down roots, takes time.

In the spring of 2013, I had a dream that I was inside the metal shed we had converted into a temple. Something was crashing against the walls, creating enormous dents, until it opened a hole and what looked like a gray octopus tentacle snaked in, pulled the walls right off. Outside, I found myself on a college campus, looking for firewood.

Sharing this dream with iishana, I was inspired to expand upon a growing awareness about the "heart seed," the seed of transcendent awareness we all carry inside, usually tightly held within the shell of the ego.

"You know the images we put on our altar? The ones we are most drawn to? Those are simply the images on our seed packages, the beings we are destined to become, just like when you buy a package of tomato or echinacea seeds. Those packages contain seeds which have the potential to become fruits or flowers, but they are not there yet. The images, the beings, we are intuitively drawn to, that we pray to, meditate before, whose images just call to us—that is where we are headed, what we intuitively know we will one day become. And the only thing holding us back is the ego—cunning, baffling and powerful— endlessly whispering our unworthiness."

At that moment, there was a knock at the door of the yurt. It was a young woman who rented a room from iishana in the main house. She was breathless. "I just remembered that I brought you guys a gift from Maui. I know how special that place is to you. Is this a good time?"

She returned with a roll of hand painted prayer flags from a retreat center on the island, like a typical set of Tibetan flags, except each one had a picture of Ganesha, the elephant-headed Hindu deity, the remover of obstacles. After she left, I wondered about my dream. I had thought it was an octopus tentacle breaking down the shed walls. Perhaps it had been a trunk?

Later that day, iishana and I headed downtown to visit *Adavasi*, the Indian store in town which had everything you might need for outfitting a temple, decorating your living room or dressing for a special event. In the window was a huge "Going out of Business" sign. We were crestfallen.

Everything had to go. Prices were slashed. All offers considered. We felt a little like vultures, but we went in anyway. In the middle of the chaos was a huge brass murti, statue, of Ganesha. He had an immense presence which commanded us to sit. As we meditated before him, iishana and I had the same thought: He was coming home with us.

Ordinarily, these kinds of objects, priced like a decent used car, are out of reach, something you gaze at, dream about. We put our heads together, made an offer, a fraction of the sticker price, and soon Ganesha was seated on the bed of my truck, heading home. We ferried him in a wheelbarrow to the very back of the yard and placed him on a large stone outcropping. Ganesha had arrived.

A year later, May of 2014, we were ready to choose a wedding date. Iishana had made it safely through her health crisis and we were still deeply in love. Ganesha's birthday, a national holiday in India, seemed like the perfect occasion. We were on our way to Cape Cod to stay with a friend when I suggested this to iishana. We had a date.

Our first morning in Truro, we had coffee outside. Seated under sweet smelling pitch pine, we eagerly planned the wedding. Later, getting ready to head out into the day, we both noticed a flash in the sand at our feet. I reached down, thinking it was a piece of aluminum. A ring came up in my hands. It was white metal, sparkling with tiny crystals. I figured it must be a piece of costume jewelry. For some reason, we kept it and brought it back to Vermont.

A couple of weeks later, I was studying the ring and noticed some marks on the inside surface. Looking closer, I read the number "750." I learned it was a marking usually used in Europe to denote gold of 75% purity, 18 karat gold. Maybe it wasn't a kid's lost ring.

At the same jewelry store where I had sold my grandparents' silver, the woman behind the counter assured me that those were real diamonds and asked if I wanted the ring appraised. I immediately called my hosts on the Cape to see if anyone had lost a ring. Someone somewhere had to be pretty bummed. "No," they replied. No missing rings.

On a whim, iishana tried it on. It fit perfectly on the fourth finger of her left hand. We stared at each other. We had been engaged to be married for almost two years, but with no specific date, an open-ended commitment. However, less than than twenty-four hours after setting a date—Ganesha's birthday—this ring had appeared. A gift from Ganesha. I was reminded of the story of Sai Baba, his hand holding the lost wedding ring, that first awakened me to the possibility of the guru: "Have you been looking for this?"

My dad turned eighty the following month and, to celebrate, he took the whole family on a cruise. All my sibs, their spouses and kids, my dad's most recent wife, Susan, and my mom. There was some precedent for this. We had, most of us, been gathering for years each summer for a week on the Cape. But this time, a few things were different.

In 2001, my dad's previous (and third) wife, Leigh, purchased a house in Onset, MA, so called because it was located at the "onset" of Cape Cod. From that year until 2010, while I was married to Tracey, annual family gatherings were held there. Even though Leigh and my dad had divorced in 1997, she remained close to me and my brothers, John and Henry, and my sister, Anne. She was estranged from her own children and saw us as surrogates. Likewise, we four kids had always been looking for a "real" mom. Leigh, with her extravagant generosity— she had bought this house so we could all get together—was the perfect stand-in for the mother we never had.

Leigh invited all four of us and our families to stay with her for a week or two every July. John, Anne and I each had two children three years apart and each set was born within a few months of one another. So when Maia was an infant, John's wife, Nora, and my sister Anne were also nursing their babies, Roan and Rebecca. And when Noah was born in May of 2004, Isla and Suzannah— Nora and Anne's baby daughters— had just arrived as potential playmates.

For ten years, we all grew and played together in Onset. It was our big yearly reunion and even though my dad was never there (he was back with his second wife, whom he would leave in 2009 for a fourth), my mom would show up on occasion for a day or two. As ex-wives of the same man, she and Leigh had a lot in common. By this time, after many years and a lot of individual therapy, all four of us kids were on friendly terms with my mother. We had no problem with this bizarre arrangement. These were happy times. Watching the young kids play together, stewarded by their older cousin, my son from my first marriage, Kirby— who was a rock star to his little half-sibs and cousins— was a joy.

These reunions ended after Tracey and I hit the rocks for the final time and Leigh was diagnosed with advanced ALS in 2010. She went into intensive care for the next eighteen months until she died. During that time, the beloved Onset house was repossessed by the bank.

My dad believed he could pick up where the rest of us had left off, this time by spending a week together on a cruise. He was turning eighty. He had a new wife. Why not give it a try? And so, on a hot muggy day in June, 2014, we all gathered on the west side of Manhattan to board the second biggest cruise ship in the world.

I was joined by iishana, whom no one in my family had yet met, and all three of my children. Henry, who hadn't married, was there as well and so was our mom. After all these years, she and my dad had settled into a pleasantly nostalgic haze, exchanging occasional phone calls and chatting in a friendly way when they overlapped at weddings and graduations. Hosting it all were my dad and his new wife, Susan. She was also a psychiatrist, and her adopted daughter, Zoe was a southern California fashion plate who had just turned twenty. She and Kirby, who worked at Armani and dressed accordingly, were poised to have the best time of any of us. The cruise ship provided endless settings for dressing up.

My entire family of origin. The six of us had not spent any real time together since my parents divorced in 1970. Now, after over forty years, we would be unable to get away from each other for a week. What could possibly go wrong?

The ship looked like an immense floating airport hotel and advertised itself as a blend of Broadway and Las Vegas. As much liquor and gambling and live entertainment as you could stand, twenty-four hours a day. And every day, a new calendar of events would be issued, titled without irony, "A Night to Remember." As soon as I stepped on board, I realized I would be trapped in a floating hell realm for the next seven days. Afterwards, when asked what it was like, iishana would reply, "You mean, the cruisifixion(sic)?"

For months before the cruise, Iishana wisely had been urging me to prepare for this floating fiasco. I pooh-poohed her every time. I was fine. It would be fun!

It was much worse than I could have imagined. Despite my having been twice blessed by Ganesha and being engaged to a wonderful woman, it had all the makings of disaster before we even left the dock. I barely had enough money to cover gas and tolls to get to the cruise ship's pier in Manhattan. When asked for a credit card number upon embarking so they could create an account for me, I had none to give them. I had defaulted eight months earlier. I wasn't going to be able to buy my kids a coke. In addition, my brother was on the cusp of publishing his third book. He was the golden boy, the "real" eldest son.

When my parents split in 1970, it was a like a clown car hitting the wall. Each of us four children, after a lifetime of abuse and neglect, was ready to come apart and the impact of divorce was all it took to spread our contents all over the street.

I started smoking cigarettes and pot, drinking heavily, by the time I was thirteen. I was selling drugs and getting suspended from school at fourteen, and spent three years at Andover just barely getting by. If it hadn't been the highly permissive seventies, I could have been kicked out several times over.

My younger brother, the future literary star, did manage to get kicked out of his prep school, but that was the least of the family's worries. His depression was so severe we feared he might not make eighteen.

My youngest brother, on the autism spectrum, attended a school for kids with disabilities. My youngest sister, Anne, was permitted no latitude for acting out; those slots were filled. She suffered quietly with anorexia.

In the years following my parents' divorce, as all us kids came completely undone, there was no therapy, no discussion. My parents were caught up in the drama of their own lives, desperate to stay afloat themselves. It was every man for himself.

And now, forty years later, after no family therapy, no opportunity to process this disaster as a group, we were reunited on a floating version of the Las Vegas strip crossbred with the Great White Way. And there certainly weren't going to be any opportunities to process on the cruise. We would be too busy having fun.

And fun there was. A free waterpark for the kids, plus soft serve ice cream machines with no adult supervision. Every wondered how high you can pile that stuff on top of a cone? There were Broadway shows, all-you-can-eat buffets, gambling around the clock. The daily calendar of events was several pages long, in small print. The only item that interested me was the "Friends of Bill's meeting," a reference to one of the founders of AA, Bill Wilson. It was an open twelve-step meeting that can be found on all cruise ships. Apparently, someone running this addicts' paradise realized it might be too much for a few unfortunates and so this one small sanctuary was set aside. I wouldn't have survived without it.

172

My recent divorce had shattered my primary means of support. How to earn money, how to be useful, how to matter to my community? These were questions I had yet to answer. Aboard a ship, sealed in the small circle of my family, these unanswered questions came under a harsh light.

My father had always been very clear that career came first. What mattered most was the mark you made. I was fifty-five years old and living in a large tent without running water.

It wasn't just the buffets that were all-you-can-eat. This family reunion provided all the material my mind needed to go full cannibal on itself. It didn't take too many family meals—my father dismissive of my ideas, my successful brother the center of attention—for me to put together enough mental tape to put myself into a clinical depression. There was nothing to do between meals except think, think about all the ways my life was a failure. No income, no accomplishments, no clear direction. These were capital offenses in my family. I had nothing to show for myself, no protection.

A therapist once observed that with me, it was all or nothing. And this was true. The few times I gambled, it was always on the longest shot. I always rooted for the underdog during the NFL playoffs. I hadn't just wanted to help create a shamanic center; I wanted to save the world. "Go big or go home" wasn't a cliché. Those were my marching orders. So if I wasn't going big…

I began to think seriously of how to jump off the boat. As I paced the decks, hoping that enough vigorous walking might take the edge off my mind's cruelty, I was also casing the stern area at all levels of the ship. Some had too many cameras. Others didn't provide a clear drop to the water. At some times of day, there were too many people. I wasn't screwing around. I was making a plan.

Just like at our reunions in Onset, the kids formed a pod, loosely supervised by the older cousins, Kirby and Susan's daughter, Zoe. Although they would check in with us parents from time to time, mostly they ran the decks, feasted at the always open buffets, and romped in the water park. They were having the best time of all of us. I was left largely free to ruminate.

I didn't share any of this with her, but iishana knew something was terribly wrong. There was just nothing she could do. She didn't know anyone in my family well enough to talk with them and I rebuffed any attempts she made to get me to open up. Didn't she know the rules of this generations-old family game? The first one to admit pain, loses.

She shared with me after the cruise how, in desperation, she had tried to find help on the ship. However, virtually the entire crew was Filipino, none with good English. After trying repeatedly to make herself understood to the ship's doctor, the steward, housekeeping, anybody!— she was finally connected to the kitchen. "Would he like something to eat?" a voice inquired in a thick accent.

My one refuge, the one respite from the self-perpetuating motion machine of my mind, was the twelve-step meeting provided each day. In there, I could talk openly about how my family was, literally, making me crazy. Everyone would smile and nod. They totally got it. Why did I think they were at the meeting?

At the time, I was wearing a single rudraksha bead around my neck. The word means "tears of Shiva" and they are traditionally worn by yogis in India. It was my connection to the guru, to Amma and Maharaj-ji. After one meeting, a young man came up and asked about it. I mentioned something about it being a connection to my spiritual teacher and he immediately responded enthusiastically about how he had just returned from India, from visiting his guru. I inquired who that might be. "Oh," the young man answered, "You probably wouldn't have heard of her. Her name is Amma."

He took out his phone and soon I was with him in India, taking a tour of Amma's ashram, seeing pictures of her feeding an elephant, hugging people. Even in the depths of this floating hell realm, Amma was here.

That evening, I received the only text I got all week, from an old friend who had just been to a Krishna Das kirtan, "Yay Maharaj-ji!" Even out here in the Atlantic Ocean, heading into the Bermuda triangle, where none of my navigational equipment was any good, my gurus were with me.

The next day, though, found me despondent again. I began to visualize jumping off the boat: finding the right time and deck, the leap into the water, the chop and froth of the big ship's wake, and, finally, just hanging there on the surface of water thousands of feet deep, the lights of the cruise ship slowly vanishing over the horizon.

In the end, it boiled down to two possibilities. First, the boat's system of cameras and alarms would register my jump, I would be rescued and brought back on board, and for the next five days, everybody would know I was the asshole who tried to ruin the cruise. Or, worse, my jump would go unnoticed. My plunge into the ocean would shock me out of my despair and I would spend the remainder of my now very short life contemplating what a terrible mistake I had just made.

Ridicule and shame or abandonment and desolation.

If I just sat for a second, felt into my worst memories, the most painful feelings I had ever experienced, they all boiled down to one or the other of these two scenarios. I was either being held up to the mirror in unbearable shame or I was crying out in the crib and no one was coming. Except this time, the person responsible was me. All my thinking, all my self-loathing, all my despair, had one purpose: to recreate, with exquisite precision and attention to detail, my worst traumas.

The coup de grace that finally quieted my mind was delivered by my stepmother's brother, from three thousand miles away. For my stepmother, Susan, it began with the worst thing you are ever likely to hear on a cruise: "We have a telephone call for you, Ma'am. It's the Orange County Police."

Our family was not alone in having its "designated patient," that family member chosen to carry the baggage, all the shit no one wants to own. In fact, in my family there was so much shit my brothers and I had to take turns playing this role. But in Susan's family, her younger brother was able to handle it on his own.

He had never been able to hold a job, dabbled continuously in a variety of illicit drugs, and was good for a dramatic blowout every couple of years. I guess it had been a while since he'd released pressure, because Susan thought it would be a good idea for him to act as caretaker for their invalid octogenarian mother while the rest of us were on the cruise.

As the Orange County police told it, the brother had gotten drunk the second day we were at sea, right when I began to seriously contemplate my big jump. And, as I was to learn later, right as my sister started to have despairing thoughts of her own and my youngest brother started to melt down, refusing to come out of his cabin. The brother had then called his son, sharing that he no longer wanted to live. Concerned, the son called the police, who immediately made a welfare check. Upon arrival, they found the brother, intoxicated, and standing over a pool of blood-colored vomit. The mother was peacefully asleep in the next room. The police took Susan's brother to a local hospital for evaluation and called her to see if there was another family member who could look after her mother. There was and the hospital released her brother soon after. However, he had fulfilled his part of the family contract; his sister's big family cruise was ruined.

And now I was going to be able to get through it in one piece. In a flash, all the urgency went out of my ferocious self-judgment. All my self-assessed "failings" felt insignificant. Like air going out of a balloon, or a painfully shrieking alarm silenced, my mind ratcheted down from DEFCON One to being mildly unhappy. The same was true for my sister and Henry.

Like some deus ex machina, like a twenty-year-old "ringer" put in during the fourth quarter of a closely contested high school football game, Susan's brother had come to the rescue. "Allow me!" he exclaimed as he swept in at the last minute to be the sacrificial lamb for our bloodthirsty family drama. Because this story demanded blood. My grandfather's suicide, my grandmother's attempted murder-suicide, had raised the bar high in this game. The family system here would not be placated by fights at the dinner table. It demanded meat: suicide threats, police intervention, hospitalization. And Susan's brother stepped up just in time.

A hurricane raged just to the west, slamming the Carolinas and leaving us to sail home through huge swells. But the rest of the trip was uneventful. As iishana and I spent the final day of the cruise sequestered in our cabin, singing kirtan before the smiling pictures of Amma and Maharaj-ji, I thought about how much they had suffered as children. Amma abused by her parents for being crazy. Maharaj-ji's mother dying when he was eight, his being driven out by his stepmother. Even the Buddha lost his mother when he was only a few days old.

I thought about how much everybody suffers. Every human being, every creature that draws breath, that has a nervous system. This sentence of life is hard labor, hard time. We all may hold on to it for "dear life," but that same life is going to cause every last one of us unimaginable pain.

As we rode across endless water, the ship heaving above massive swells from a storm that had only just missed us, I knew why the oceans are filled with salt water. It's from all the tears. Shed by billions of creatures' suffering over millions of years, this pain fills our seas. Want to know how much it hurts to be alive? Just look at the world's oceans, covering most of the planet's surface under salt water several miles deep.

No one gets a reprieve. No one gets out alive. And while we may natter and squabble about all the tiny details on the surface, every little white cap and eddy, underneath us, holding all of us up, connecting the whole world, are unspeakably large volumes of pain. It's what we share. It's what connects us. And when we finally surrender to this simple fact, open our arms to one another with the immense embrace of one who really sees, really gets that the other's suffering is no different from our own, we will have finally arrived at our true home, joined our true family.

Chapter 14

Unobscured Radiance

Back on dry land, my internal compass continued to swing wildly. Everything had been clear before; the shaman's path became so obvious and then flowed seamlessly into the way of the guru. I was reminded of my early journey to discover my soul's purpose—when Michael Harner and Sandra Ingerman, threw me out of the helicopter over the Badlands. Maharaj-ji and Amma had tossed me out of my old life, too, but this time there wasn't a medicine man pointing me towards a vision quest. This time there was silence.

Even marrying iishana felt like a bad idea. I was lost. I had no clear means of support, no clear purpose or direction. And then the phone rang.

It was my buddy, Elliot. We were brothers on the spiritual path. Like Rod, he was a year older than me and had gotten out of the urban rat race shortly after college and had been homesteading ever since, far from his Long Island roots. He was deeply connected with the Brattleboro "alternative community" (artists, activists, farmers, spiritual seekers) and had taken me under his wing shortly after I arrived in town. We were both Amma devotees, but today he had something else on his mind.

Some *ayahuasceros*, shamans skilled in the use of the powerful rain forest hallucinogen, were in the area. Did I want to join him on a "medicine journey"? Ayahuasca has very much come into vogue at this time and is widely reported on in the media. However, my connection with this powerful teaching plant went back decades. I had never taken it, but considered it an important part of my spiritual lineage. It is what woke Michael Harner up, inspired him to develop the shamanic drumming method which changed the course of my life.

So when my friend invited me to drink from the sacred vine, I paused. For one thing, ayahuasca can in no way be termed a "recreational" drug. It means business. Having drunk a medium-sized dose of the brew, you can expect to vomit for hours. The stuff cleans you out, stem to stern. Like the man said, "You can't be a hollow bone if you're full of shit." In order to receive teachings this powerful, this important, you damn well better have "beginner's mind."

Just the same, I was stuck. None of my navigational systems were working. Ayahuasca seemed like a good idea. Time to return to my roots.

That night, in a large tipi, thirty of us sat quietly in a circle around the central fire. The people leading the ceremony, a couple from Brazil, silently called each of us in turn to come and drink the brew. The flavor is hard to describe. A friend of mine who has been to the Amazon several times, says it is something like cigar butts mixed with burned grapefruit rind. "Not too far off," I thought as I chugged the cupful I was given.

That night was Guru Purnima, the full moon of the guru, the night it is believed in India that the guru is a thousand times closer than on any other night, a night when her grace pours over you just like the silvery moon was pouring through the smoke hole of the tipi. However, to

Damiana and David, the Brazilian shamans guiding us, this information was irrelevant. We were working with Santo Daime, Saint Ayahuasca. That was all we needed to know.

As the night went on, some people curled up in their sleeping bags while others danced around the fire. By another coincidence, the music our hosts played included the kirtan of Krishna Da, a longtime Maharaj-ji devotee. As he sang to Hanuman, one of the dancers became Hanuman in my eyes, the perfect devotee, offering himself up to Ram, lord of all the gods. We were now in Ram's durbar, the god's royal court, in heaven, everything and everyone illuminated by pulsing silver light. We were divine beings, bathed in perfection.

As I rose to dance, two objects came into my mind, floated before me, messages from God. I saw the diamond ring iishana and I had found two months before in Truro, floating and sparkling in the firelight, a gift from Ganesha himself. And I saw the rudraksha bead I was wearing as the original Heart Seed, which only needed to be planted, tended carefully, in order to sprout into the Tree of Life, "the wish-fulfilling tree" sung of in the Vedas. Neither the ring nor the seed was an "object" any longer. Something inside them was now shining inside me, showing me the way.

I had my coordinates. As if on a mountain top that rises above clouds, I could see clearly, knew which way to go. It might be murky down below, back in the ordinary world, but I knew if I continued with the wedding plans, continued to cultivate the heart seed, I would not, could not, go wrong. The sense of relief was immense. My navigation system was back online. The joy which had guided me this far was once again shining clearly and brightly. Something true and good to lead me, something true and good to follow.

Soon after, iishana and I began to host the monthly Amma satsangs she had been guided to offer two years earlier. From then on, we hosted fellow devotees every month in song, prayer and meditation. The saying, "when two or more gather, I am there," is not just a Christian principle.

Amma was now visiting us every month in the form of satsang, gathering of truth seekers. The guru was not simply a being we saw once a year. She had a room in our house.

A few weeks after the ayahuasca ceremony, iishana and I were married. One of the happiest days of my life. We celebrated Ganesha's birthday with fifty friends and family on a bright sunny late August day full of music, song, story and ceremony. My mother and father were both there, but this time no one regressed into the "bad old days." Iishana's and my true parents— Amma and Maharaj-ji— were the hosts and the incredible joy they suffused was felt by everyone.

One of our first acts as a newly married couple was to begin a serious tantric practice. At first, this simply meant getting to know each other sensually without the goal of orgasm. For me, lovemaking always had a clear objective—the "money shot" of ejaculation. Wonderful as this is, the prospect of coming meant my attention was rarely in the present moment. Letting go of this peak experience felt like a sacrifice at first, but it opened up new worlds.

Over the following months, iishana's and my connection deepened steadily as our physical intimacy lost its transactional nature. We were no longer in the "business" of exchanging orgasms. We were learning to love each other without any conditions, any expectations. In turn, because our attention was no longer focused on the blast of climax, our senses, our energy experiences became subtler and more refined.

Even after just two months of these "exchanges," I became aware of the most exquisite energy spectrums vibrating between us. I also became aware of how much orgasm-centered sex had informed the rest of my life, how often I focused on end results rather than upon each moment of Now, where I actually was.

Intensifying this growing awareness, a bumper sticker caught my eye as I was coming out of the grocery store:

I am one epiphany short of a paradigm shift.

Not long after, I took my daughter, who had changed her name from Maia to Nix, to the Museum of Fine Arts in Boston. Nix was thirteen and having a rough time. She was the same age my brother and I had been when we first plunged into bouts of severe depression. One bright spot was her passion for art and, again just as mine had been at thirteen, her eye was caught by the joy of the Impressionists, especially the radiant colors of Monet.

It was late December, but stepping into the Rabb Gallery, with its thirty-foot ceilings and huge skylight, was like entering an immense sun-splashed conservatory. Instead of tropical plants, this space was filled with dozens of brilliantly colored paintings, their lambent light accentuated by gray damask walls. Nix immediately gravitated toward the Monets—paintings of the Rouen Cathedral, the eponymous Haystacks, scenes of the Mediterranean. As she basked in their glow, she came alive—happier, more talkative. As her knowledge of the painter's technique and history poured out, I was no longer with a sullen thirteen-year old, but a joyful and passionate young woman.

I didn't want the day to end and neither did Nix, but it was time to go. As we headed toward the museum exit, she stopped me. "But Dad, we only saw what I wanted to see. Is there a gallery you want to visit?"

There was. Thanks to Boston's wealthy Yankee traders and their clipper ships to the Orient, the MFA has an extraordinary East Asian collection. A highlight is the Temple Room, designed in 1909 to evoke the contemplative atmosphere of a Buddhist temple. As we entered the dark and silent space, shadowy Buddhas of all sizes emerged out of the gloom. Huge time-darkened cedar beams framed the space and I could feel my breathing, my heartbeat, slow. We were no longer in busy 2014 Boston, but in a much older place where silence was power.

I was drawn to an immense seated Buddha—Amida, the Buddha of Infinite Light—carved from Japanese cypress in the twelfth century. Even sitting, he was easily five feet tall, eyes downcast, hands together in a mudra. There were only a few minutes before the Museum closed, but, as I sat before him, my eyes drawn to the small crystal at the center of his forehead, I felt an immense gravitational pull. It was as if this seated figure carried centuries of meditation and devotion within him—the concentration of countless monks stored in this small shining stone, suspended in a dark ocean of wood—and I was somehow included in this mystery.

While I sat, bathed in this being's light, Nix waited patiently at the side of the room, much as a kind older relative waits for a boy in a toy store. For a moment, our roles were reversed and my daughter was curating my transcendent experience.

We did not speak of this on the way home, but I was reminded of the presence she revealed at age four, when she told me she was an artist. Beneath the storms of adolescence ran much deeper waters. There was a profound shared knowing here, not only a shared depression, but an even deeper appreciation of the power of light. I learned later that Amida's great attribute was the ability to turn longing into limitless light. Just as Monet had done for my daughter that afternoon.

I learned about Amida in a book I 've returned to over and over, The Tibetan Book of Living and Dying. The author, Sogyal Rinpoche, suggests that

Only by going over this book and reading it again and again...can its many layers of meaning be revealed...(and) you will come to realize the depth of the wisdom that is being transmitted to you... (14)

Indeed, every time I picked this book up it took me deeper.

After my split with Tracey, I put this book down. I had other things to think about. But before our trip to Boston, Nix and I had gone with Noah and iishana to visit her sister. Shortly after we arrived, Nix emerged from the bathroom. "Hey, Dad," she said. "Look what I found in the trash." She was holding a copy of *The Tibetan Book of Living and Dying*, discarded by a previous guest. Evidently, it was time to resume my studies.

As I worked again with this book, there was a quote from one of the author's principle teachers, Dudjom Rinpoche, which kept resonating:

Having purified the great delusion, the heart's darkness, the radiant light of the unobscured sun continually rises. (349)

Sogyal repeats this quote several times through the course of The Tibetan Book of Living and Dying. Clearly it is very important. But what does it mean? How is it to be accomplished?

A few weeks after encountering that unusual bumper sticker, "I am one epiphany short of a paradigm shift," the missing epiphany revealed itself.

Humans really face only one problem, Eckhart Tolle tells us, compulsive thinking. It's not that there is anything wrong with thinking per se. Just as there is nothing wrong with trowels or televisions. But if we use them constantly, without interruption, believing they hold the answer to all our problems, that is a problem.

In turn, because we think constantly, believing that thinking can solve all challenges, we come to believe our thoughts, see them as real, and, in turn, respond to them as such. This is the essence of "civilization," of literate, urban, pyramidally-organized society. It wasn't that people didn't think before. It's just that tribal people faced an incontrovertible challenge to the hegemony of thought—nature. No matter how real you thought your thoughts were, the natural world had the final word.

However, with the advent of agriculture on a large scale and the accumulation of immense grain surpluses, humans began to believe they could have the final word. And, in turn, thoughts grew ever more powerful, creating pyramids, cities and armies, laws and social classes—incontrovertible "proof" of private property and inequality. The world of mind had begun and, like a virus, replicating itself without regard for its host's survival, has come to surround and engulf the planet.

It has been said, "The mind is a wonderful tool and a terrible master." The Buddha said, "All life is suffering." And the engine of this suffering is what we think about life, what we become attached to and what we are averse to.

The solution, however, is simple, the Buddha tells us. As does Patanjali, the historical founder of Yoga: Meditate. Of course, that raises all kind of questions and libraries have been filled with answers. But it all boils down to two words: Stop thinking.

Or as Jamyang Khyentse once told a devotee, "Look, it's like this. When the past thought has ceased, and the future thought has not arisen, isn't there a gap?"

"Yes," the devotee replied.

"Well, prolong it. That is meditation." (75)

That gap, tiny and brief as it is at first, is the key to liberation. As we gradually learn to stop thinking all the time, when we learn to still our mind instead of letting it ride roughshod over us, we gain our freedom. What torments us constantly, what imprisons us, taxes us, abuses us, is almost entirely our own thinking. My mother was abusive to me in my childhood, but who has abused me ceaselessly for over half a century, torn my marriages apart, come close on several occasions to convincing me to end my life?

And so, in an instant, on a February morning in 2015, I was able to complete Dudjom Rinpoche's intriguing promise, adding (in bold) ten words to explain it and a sentence after to clarify:

When we embrace the emptiness of the gap between thoughts, we purify the great delusion, the heart's darkness, and allow the radiance of the unobscured sun to continually shine. We discover the bliss of being, the true nature of mind.

My mind stopped for a moment. A glowing began at the center of my chest, radiating, expanding outward in ripples of gold, until I felt enclosed in a sphere of light. I had to go outside, move my body. The feeling of radiance was almost too intense to bear. Walking along the brook which ran near my house, my attention would begin to wander back into thinking. All I had to do was repeat the words which had just come to me. Like hitting the "off" switch. My thoughts were replaced by the same blissful, golden glow, quietly throbbing through my entire body.

Every time we are able to embrace the emptiness of the gap between our thoughts, allow ourselves to rest for a moment in the mind's silence, we purify the "great delusion"—the belief that our thoughts are real. Mental quiet, like a cool cloth on a fevered brow, soothes our inflamed minds, stops us from continually aggravating our own anxiety, depression, anger. Those thoughts— "like clouds," countless Buddhist texts say—darken our world, shade us from the sunlight of our own hearts. Just like we can forget the sun exists on a cloudy day, begin to lose hope after a stretch of such days, our unceasing and unquestioned thinking makes us forget who we are.

A few months later, iishana and I were with Amma again in Marlborough, where she comes every year to embrace her New England devotees. As we walked through the crafts bazaar which always accompanied her, I kept being drawn to a large cotton batik of the emblem of her ashram, an enormous sun at the center. The joyful radiance of this image captured the inner radiance I was feeling more and more frequently. More than any words, this image represented, no <u>was</u>, ananda, the joy which lay beneath all reality.

Studying the batik in our hotel room, I noticed a banner beneath the sun, bearing words written in Sanskrit. Back home, I learned the English meaning of these words, "By renunciation alone is immortality attained." Amma's motto. Words to set you free.

"Renunciation" is a hard word for us. Giving things up. It sounds like punishment. We don't give things up here in America. We get more and more.

Jamyang Khentse had said to his devotee that the only way to enter "gap" between thoughts was to give up—renounce— thinking, even if only for a second or two. The "renunciation" Amma was gently pointing us toward wasn't about quitting everything we liked to eat or drink; it was about giving up thinking all the time.

I was curious whether this motto was original to Amma or if it came from an older source. I was led to the Kaivalyopanishad, the ancient Upanishad (traditional Hindu texts about how to achieve liberation) which told of how to achieve kaivalya, oneness with all existence. I ordered a translation of this text and, a few days later, it was in my hands.

I had awoken before iishana and was sitting in my favorite chair enjoying my first cup of coffee while I read. I only got as far as the second stanza. As in all the Upanishads, (a word whose root comes from the Sanskrit for "sitting near," as in "near the feet of the Master"), the text begins as the student approaches the guru and asks to be liberated. Here the student is Asvalayana, a famous teacher of the *Rig Veda*, the root Hindu text, and his teacher is Brahma, God himself.

Asvalyana wants to know how to reach *paraatparam purusha*, the highest truth of all, the knowing which unlocks all creation and sets you free. The commentary explains this term by breaking it into pieces. *Purusha* comes from the Sanskrit for Self or Consciousness. *Para* is unmanifest. *Apara* is manifest, as in the English, "apparent." Using the analogy of a tree, the commentator explains that the fully grown tree is apara, what you can easily see, and the tree's seed is *para*, not obviously a tree, but containing its possibility.

The commentary then explains that the *apara purusha* is the visible manifestation of all creation, whereas the *parapurusha* is the seed or potential or root cause of all creation. At this point, I feel a glowing, pulsating vibration in my heart center. This place at the center of my being, this feeling of original joy, this place my hand has been resting thanks to Maharaj-ji's guidance, the place Ramana Maharshi points to when he says he knows who he is. This heart center is what iishana and I have been talking about when we talk about the Heart Seed.

This place, at the very center of my being, at the very center of Being, is the paraatparam purusha. I don't need to continue reading. Never mind finding Amma's motto in the text. The answer is right here, right now. As I am sitting there, reeling at the magnitude of what I have been shown, iishana sits bolt upright in bed, ten feet away.

"I just had this amazing dream," she said. "I have to share it before I forget. It explains how the guru works, how she does what she does." Iishana went on to describe a figure all in white, sitting cross legged, while a devotee stands before her. The same scene described in the book I was holding.

"There is a stream of light coming from behind the figure in white. It enters her right behind her heart center where it is transformed. This new light then pours out from the guru's chest, striking the devotee at the center of his chest, in turn transforming his atoms. And that's how the guru works. That's how she transforms us." She paused, "The vibration of hydrogen, that's what it is. The vibration of hydrogen. It enters the guru and the guru shines it out of her heart. That's what it is. The vibration of hydrogen."

Hydrogen *is* the physical form of *paraatparam purusha*, the seed of all creation, the source of all the other elements. As mystical cosmologist, Brian Swimme, observes,

Take hydrogen and leave it alone. After a while it becomes rosebushes and giraffes and human beings.

The apparent version of this wisdom is the world we can see. But the secret, hidden version of hydrogen is its capacity to create everything out of nothing, the omnipresent force of love which unconditionally allows us to exist. When you experience this truth with the surrendered heart of the guru, you know, feel with your whole body, that everything is unconditional love. Living from this place of joyful awareness, you can transform others so as to be able to do likewise. This transformational awareness is the secret of the universe!

I floated out of the yurt and headed for work. I'd found a gig as a carpenter with a team of younger men, half of whom had some kind of connection to Whitey Bulger, the recently arrested Boston gangster. Not an especially yogic bunch. But it paid the bills, worked my body hard enough that the celibacy required by our tantric practice was manageable.

Later that same day, I was putting the finishing touches on some built-in cabinets when the homeowners, retired seventy-somethings, came into the room. "Look," the woman said, "We are already putting them to use." She opened one of the doors to reveal an immense quartz crystal, bigger than my head. "My husband found this in a cave in South Dakota."

I was taken back to the journey I had gone on twenty years before—searching for my soul's original purpose. In that journeying, I had been thrown out of a helicopter over the Badlands, fallen through layers of stone into a cave. My spirit teacher, the old blind Lakota medicine man, sat shining in the darkness, pointing me towards the vision quest where I would have my first glimpse of ananda. Jung would have said this old man was the Self, the concentrated crystalline awareness which lies at the center of consciousness.

"Did you find this near Pine Ridge?" I asked, referring to the Oglala Lakota reservation

The woman's husband looked suddenly self-conscious. "Uh, yes. How did you know?"

I felt little dizzy. In Tibetan Buddhism, when the master gives transmission of a core teaching, he will often show the disciple a quartz crystal at the moment of revelation to illustrate the "clear light" of the mind. Being shown this immense crystal the morning I'd first experienced *paraatparam purusha* had exactly the same effect. Here, in physical form, was combined, in three of my spiritual lineages, the essential nature of mind which I had first been shown twenty years before and had been tracking ever since.

In a single moment, everything combined into One: My original question about my soul's purpose twenty years before and the Lakota spirit teacher who had guided me to my first experience of *ananda*. The Tibetan tradition— my connection to Jamyang Khyentse and the bodhisattva of wisdom, Manjushri, the experience of liberation at the *Rigpa* center in Ireland. My Indian gurus, Amma and Maharaj-ji— the essence of the Upanishads revealed that morning in the yurt. My entire quest of over two decades, the myriad traditions and teachers I had been led to—all became this single moment, this glimpse of the biggest crystal I had ever seen. It twinkled in the cupboard, clear points extending in all directions, silvery grey in its valleys, shining brilliantly where its peaks and edges caught the sun. Everything got kind of wavery and I couldn't speak. The three of us stood there in silence.

And then the homeowner shut the cabinet door and I went back to spackling nail holes. Like that, Life was revealed and then the door of ordinary appearances closed upon it. Like when I first held Kirby in my arms, felt Life and Death and God all crowded in the little room along with Nancy and the midwife, an energy so big it could blow the world to pieces. And then it was just a hospital room again and I had a baby to take care of, something I knew nothing about.

Chapter 15

The Most Powerful Force in the Universe

The following year, in June of 2016, iishana and I made a pilgrimage to Maharaj-ji's ashram in Taos, New Mexico. Although he never came to America, the grounds of his ashram were suffused with his presence. Iishana and I arrived there separately, but we were both in tears within minutes. For me, the moment came in the temple where, in addition to an enormous marble murti of a flying Hanuman, a replica of Maharaj-ji's takhat (Sanskrit for "throne" or "seat") had been set up along one wall. It was a narrow cot covered with one of the guru's legendary plaid blankets, his only possession. When I arrived, another devotee was kneeling before it, her head laid sideways on the blanket. Although this seemed a little much— the man had never even been here— I figured it was the way of the place and knelt by the bed after the woman left.

No sooner had my cheek touched the rough wool of my guru's blanket then my eyes filled with tears. I saw, felt, my own longings as a boy for a just and peaceful world, remembered my first awareness of poverty, how cruelly unfair it was. Of course, I soon learned that such childish hopes were exactly that, childish, and that I would have to learn to accept suffering as part of the world's package.

The large photograph of Maharaj-ji above the bed caught my eye. Light poured out of his face. His eyes shone and his smile scooped me up in an enormous embrace. He had never accepted such suffering. He had never let go of this "childish" dream. In fact, this longing to relieve human suffering had grown within him, becoming increasingly powerful over decades, until now, forty years after his death, it had acquired an intensity which was almost frightening. There was a golden light pouring out of his being which bore down on human suffering like a category 5 hurricane, splintering trees and flattening houses, all our illusions about how things are. This radiance which emanated from him was annihilation by joy, an immense wave of unconditional love, bigger than anything you could imagine.

And in his radiant power, I felt an affirmation of my little boy dream. He knew exactly what had hurt my heart all those years ago—injustice—the powerful taking advantage of and abusing the weak: a brutal imbalance infecting all human interaction, from the smallest—parent and child—to the largest—the tectonic grinding of social classes and nation states. And he had dedicated his life, his entire being, to healing this terrible human wound, to setting us free. And this dedication was not in any way poignant or touching, the way we might feel about some long-suffering charity worker. It was enormous, magnificent, unstoppable. I saw why C.S. Lewis would choose to depict Christ as a lion in the Narnia Chronicles. What Maharaj-ji was, what he sought tirelessly to awaken in us, was not tender or frail. It was golden and ferocious.

I knelt and wept for long minutes as this new knowing poured over me. Here was a man who knew what was in my heart, even when I was a boy, and knew that what I most longed for was not weakness or naivete, but a source of the most extraordinary power.

A day or two after our return, iishana and I attended a yoga class taught by a dear friend and fellow Amma devotee, Tracy Donahue. Her yoga studio was more like a temple than a fitness center and her way of teaching was reminiscent of a priestess. We had reached the end of the class and were all lying in shivasana when I saw in my mind's eye a cluster of words coming down toward me from the ceiling, a message from Maharaj-ji.

The most powerful force in the universe is the surrendered heart.

2017 found me steady on the surface, but uneasy below. On the whole, life was good. I had taken root in Brattleboro. Iishana and I were living in my yurt in her back yard (her actual house was filled with renters) and I was earning enough money to pay my bills. Adjunct teaching had picked up and I also had a part time job as the building manager of the local art museum. iishana and I were happy together. Although we had slacked a little with our tantric practice, it was working for us. Life without orgasm seemed ok.

It started while I was walking our dog, a rescue from Tennessee who had joined us a few months before. Something about a man with a dog, while not quite as irresistible as a man with a baby, seems to put women at ease, makes them a lot more likely to smile at you, start a conversation.

Emily lived on the next block, along my dog walking route, and I often saw her sitting on her front steps while she had a cigarette. At first, it would just be a friendly hello, pleasantries about the weather, but one day I asked for a smoke.

Emily was an artist in her late twenties, beautiful in a quiet way, shy where iishana was bright and outgoing. That's how it always started. Whatever woman I was with, there was always someone else who had qualities on the other side of the wheel. Emily loved to read, poetry especially. Mary Oliver was her favorite.

A ritual began. She wasn't always on her steps when I walked Little Bear, but often she was and then I would ask for a cigarette and we would chat for a few minutes, sometimes about Mary Oliver, other times

195

about our shared love for the woods. She was not overtly spiritual, another contrast with iishana, but the way she loved nature was implicitly mystical. She could lose herself with her easel in a sea of ferns or along the bank of a stream.

I spend a lot of time remembering, recalling, reviewing, almost like telling a rosary, rubbing each bead of memory between the fingers of my thoughts until it is smooth and pleasing. So while the actual amount of time I spent with Emily could be counted in minutes, the time I spent thinking about her stretched into hours.

I knew such rumination could lead to problems. The more you think about anything, the more real it becomes, taking on a life of its own. And such recollections become all too easily augmented with fantasy, imagining where a particular moment could have gone, a little like germinating seeds.

It was also like taking a drink or a drug. In fact, as I selected particularly sweet moments with Emily, ran them through my mind, polishing and refining them, imagining where they could have gone if we had chatted a little longer, I could feel my internal chemistry responding, almost as if I were behind the counter in a pharmacy after hours. By selecting particular thoughts, rewinding and replaying specific memories, augmenting them with just the right amount of fantasy, I could become literally intoxicated, exalted and poisoned, by the workings of my mind.

And so began a familiar game: longing, moving toward the longing with my thoughts, and then backing away with recrimination, then succumbing to the now "forbidden" thinking. I was in a self-seductive dance with my thoughts about Emily, just as I had been with women before her, just as I could be with alcohol or cigarettes or pot. In twelve-step programs, this is called "stinking thinking," or "romancing the drink."

One week, our fingers would brush as I accepted a cigarette, another week our gaze would hold, her large green eyes locking with mine. Then

I might not see her for a month, just think about her, editing and splicing remembered moments into an intoxicating film loop, a preview of coming attractions.

I knew this was completely fucked up. I started going to twelve-step meetings again. Not because I wanted a drink, but because my feelings about Emily were threatening to become "unmanageable." This kind of screwing around had wrecked my first two marriages.

But this wasn't something you could talk about in a meeting. The program was about alcohol and drugs. I changed my dog walking route, avoided going by Emily's house whenever I thought she might be around.

My connection with iishana was deep. I had no desire to leave her. Our shared connection with Amma, in particular, was especially precious to me, my spiritual foundation. It was just that there was a more primal longing that only Emily promised to touch.

Iishana and I continued to hold Amma satsangs in our home every month. We had a regular group of fellow devotees including a woman, Eleni, who not only looked just like Amma, but was a gifted singer and musician, whose day job was teaching music to troubled kids in the drug and gang-ravaged towns of Holyoke and Springfield in Massachsetts. It was Eleni who first suggested we sing for Amma.

Wherever Amma went, she was accompanied by constant *bhajan*, devotional singing. Most was performed by the devotees from her ashram in India, who accompany her on her round-the-world tours. But they needed a break to eat and sleep, so when they were off duty, devotees from regional satsangs were permitted to perform, usually in the wee hours. Just the idea that our little Brattleboro group could aspire to such a level—to sing for our guru in front of hundreds of people—seemed farfetched, but Eleni specialized in miracles. Her day job, after all, was pushing, cajoling, inspiring at-risk kids to play violins and clarinets.

So for the past couple of years, she had guided us through endless rehearsals until we were ready to sing for Amma for twenty minutes at around three in the morning. This year, Eleni wanted me to sing lead and for it to be a song of my own composition.

The song, whose lyrics came to me during the three-day sweat lodge back in 2007, whose melody was downloaded on a subsequent silent meditation retreat, had really touched Eleni. She could play it on her harmonium and had composed a violin part. And now she wanted me to sing it for Amma.

I am held. I am healed. I am whole. I am holy. I am home.

I would have the whole satsang with me, but she wanted me to sing the first verse a capella.

We all have family myths and perhaps the most tenacious in mine was that men can't sing. I had been certifiably tone deaf since birth and although twelve years of marriage to Tracey had taught me to sing in tune most of the time, for me to start a song by myself on key was an uncertain proposition. Nevertheless, Eleni was determined. She had coaxed music out of much harder cases.

It took three tries before I hit the right note. When we finished our performance, an endless three minutes later, people actually applauded, came up to me afterward. Eleni was truly a miracle worker.

An hour after we sang that night, at around four in the morning, I went up for my hug. Usually Amma only holds people for a few seconds. Each evening, there are thousands of people in line and, even with such brief hugs, she will remain on stage well into the following morning. However, when my turn came, she drew me into her emerald sari and held on. She murmured in my ear for a moment in Malalayam, "Madura,

198

Madura," so sweet, so sweet, and then continued her multiple conversations with others around her—giving mantras, answering logistical questions from her swamis, casual chitchat—but she did not let go of me. For what felt like minutes, all motion in the great hall ceased as I was drawn deeper and deeper into her rose-infused embrace. I had been getting hugs from Amma for years, but this single one extended beyond all the others combined.

I knew she knew everything about me, knew of my devotion and my lapses, knew of my struggle with my feelings for Emily, my shame. And I knew that every once in a while, she would give a particular devotee a hug like this. I had always wondered why, why she had chosen that specific person for a hug that hung in time, thousands of devotees suspended around her. I thought of Dattan the leper, that remarkable day when he was the focus of her attention. And now it was me.

Two weeks later, I took my son, Noah, up to Baxter State Park in Maine to climb Mt. Katahdin. Memories of hikes with my dad were strong in my mind. I wanted to give my son a taste of the grandeur of the mountains my father had given me. We had climbed nearby Monadnock a couple of times in previous years, but Noah was thirteen now, ready for something bigger than a day hike.

We went out for five days. Noah impressed me with his vigor and initiative. He hiked like a man and I told him so. Up at Chimney Pond, the glacial lake nestled beneath the thousand-foot cliffs of Katahdin's summit, I presented him with a folding Buck knife, a walnut-handled, brass-edged heirloom much like the one my father gave me at that age. He was growing up, making me proud, and I wanted him to have a talisman. But even in this refuge, Emily disturbed my dreams. I awoke the second morning out and could feel where she had been stroking my cheek.

Things didn't get better after I returned to Brattleboro and reached a head after a twelve-step meeting where the group spent an hour discussing the Fifth Step— to share one's "fearless moral inventory" with another human being. The core message of this step is brutal: "You are as sick as your secrets." As I left the meeting that day, this truth was pressing in on me hard, like a big hand pushing down on my head. I had to tell somebody about Emily.

I settled upon a former therapist, "Father Joe," I liked to call him, a gifted psychologist who once considered the priesthood. I would make my confession to him.

Sitting in his office, I felt stupid and ashamed. I was a serious seeker, a would-be spiritual teacher, struggling with a schoolboy crush. It was hard to get the words out, but not nearly as hard as hearing what Father Joe had to say.

"You need to tell iishana."

In his experience, people in a marriage for "the long haul" needed to make a clean breast of things if they wanted to last.

"No way."

This kind of gratuitous honesty was a nonstarter. I knew from painful experience where that went.

But the longing continued. I returned to my old dog walking route, began to run into Emily again, share smokes and secrets. Our fingers brushed with more intention when she passed me cigarettes, our gaze held for longer moments. I was thinking about her all the time.

Talking to my therapist didn't help. I shared everything with him, told him it was still under control, that the hand grenade wasn't going to go off.

"It sounds like you have already pulled the pin."

Fantasies about Emily tormented me. I replayed endless mental tape and envisioned scenarios where I didn't continue on my walk with Little Bear, but followed her up to her apartment. It wasn't clear what happened after that but I knew if I crossed her threshold, I wasn't coming back.

The old addictive dance between longing and self-recrimination intensified. The more I wanted Emily, the more I beat myself up. The more I beat myself up, the more I wanted her. As I rode this terrible roller coaster, I stared out at the mountains across the river. They reminded me of Amma's immense green embrace.

Emily called to me from her perch on the steps. She held her laptop. "Want to see my favorite caterpillar?"

Who could resist? I went up to her, leaned close as she showed me images on the screen. I was careful not to make contact as I knelt beside her, but the gravitational pull was strong. I felt dizzy.

She was showing me images of the "camouflaging looper," an unusual species of caterpillar that hides itself from predators by catching flower petals in its spiky coat, adorning itself all in red or purple or blue, like an undulating flower. I had never seen such a thing.

Later, as I continued on my dog walk, I was struck by the unusual name: "Camouflaging looper." This was the perfect description of what I was suffering from. The desperate "unique" longing I felt for Emily was precisely the feeling which led me to kiss Kiera, led me to cheat on my first wife so many times. As I looked back across my life, I had been sucked in again and again to shameful and destructive behavior by this same urgent feeling which brooked no argument. And each time, this feeling had camouflaged itself as being unique and new, never before seen or experienced. A once-in-a-lifetime opportunity!

I followed this trail back across the decades until I was pushing open a hidden door, creeping down a concrete hallway, pulling down my pants. This dance I was in with Emily was no different than my dance with shit fifty years before. I might be telling myself what a beautiful woman she was, what a profound connection we shared, how I had to have her, but all I was doing was slowly pulling open that long ago door, lost in the same poisonous longing, endlessly repeating, "looping," camouflaged each time by a new and enticing disguise.

And while I may not have known what lay behind that door when I was five, I could not claim ignorance now. I had the wreckage of two marriages, the near unbearable pain of leaving my children, twice. And, of course, it would be no different this time. Another marriage trashed, another carefully created community damaged. I would be covering myself with shit once again, but this time, as with all the times before, except one, my mother would have nothing to do with it.

That afternoon, I went to visit an old friend. Mark Morey was a passionate outdoor educator and visionary who sees our connection with nature as the solution to humanity's collective madness. That day, he was holding a strange object in his hand. It looked like some kind of organic bathroom fixture. It had a stem just like a shower head and opened out like a funnel. Its three-inch face was perforated with holes about half an inch in diameter which looked like outlets for the spray.

"What do you think it is?" he asked.

I had no idea.

"It's the seed pod of a water lily. You can see the seeds through these openings."

I could see them lurking below the pod's surface, the size and color of shelled acorns.

"And these seeds can last a thousand years. They can still be germinated after all that time."

My mind spun. A water lily. The North American equivalent of a lotus, the flower Buddha had held up in his famous "Flower Sermon." On that long ago day, the Buddha was at his wit's end. Unable, after thirteen years of lecturing, to awaken any of his disciples, he realized the time for talking was over. That day, instead of giving his usual lecture, he held up a flower. And for one disciple, that's all it took. The vision of the Buddha holding a lotus in silence, so unbearably beautiful yet so fleeting, had cracked open his understanding of impermanence and, in that moment, Mahakasyapa achieved liberation.

And here, my friend was offering a fresh take on that same teaching. This wise man was sitting silently, holding the dried husk of what had once been a beautiful flower, and yet here an even deeper preciousness was revealed: a thousand years after that flower bloomed and withered, everyone then living turned to dust, something remained which, if conditions were right, would not just produce another flower, but could seed an entire lake with such blooms. I was being shown the deeper implications of impermanence, the immortality which lay beneath.

Later that day, I was walking past Emily's house and this time I did not have Little Bear. He would have gotten in the way. Emily wasn't on her steps, but I was pretty sure she was home. This time I wasn't waiting until next time. This time I was going up the steps, across the porch, ringing her bell, and then ringing it a second time. I was sick of this bullshit back and forth in my head. This time I was going to find out what was real.

There is a line in the Twelve Promises (a less well-known companion of the Twelve Steps), the twelfth and final promise, that "We will suddenly come to realize that God was doing for us what we could not do for ourselves." Emily didn't answer the door. I'd been spared

When I got home, though, I still planned to follow through. I knew that, eventually, she would answer the door, and whatever we had not yet been able to say to each other would be said. And I knew, from the slowly lengthening finger brushes, longer shared gazes, exactly where that would lead.

But, like any good addict, my endless fantasies about Emily never included what came after. I had never "thought the drink through." So when I came back into the yurt that day, I was surprised to notice something had changed. I couldn't see it, couldn't touch it, but there was a wall between iishana and me. Even though I had yet to formally violate my vows to my wife, the power of my intention was suddenly palpable. And, worse, I could sense that iishana felt it, too. We didn't say anything, nothing had changed on the surface. But everything was a fraction of an inch, a millisecond, from being completely different forever.

Singing kirtan with her didn't help. As we sang the familiar words—praises to Ganesha, pleas to Krishna, gratitude to Kali—the melodies were flat. Who was I kidding? All this devotion, all the beautiful paintings and murtis in our yurt which made many people feel like they were entering a temple? I could feel the terrible choice surface in my guts—the sudden, overwhelming pleasure of connecting physically with Emily or the much longer, slower, subtler glow of my connection to iishana and to our spiritual community. I could not have both.

I lay in bed that night, unable to sleep. I was being torn in two.

The next morning, I left early. The less false interaction with iishana, the better. It was too early to ring Emily's doorbell so I settled on the next best thing. A twelve-step meeting. It wasn't one I usually went to and I arrived late, never a good sign. The topic did not interest me and everyone who spoke seemed dull and stupid. Why was I even here? But my mind would not be silenced, a good thing for once.

It started with math. How many hours did I spend with iishana and how many would I be likely to spend with Emily when we began our affair? I broke it down by week. 168 hours in seven days. If I saw Emily for a couple of hours every week or two, that would be two hours of unimaginable ecstasy against the rest my life. As I considered those two hours with Emily, I could feel they would be almost too intense, like a snort of meth. And as for the rest of those hours, forget getting any sleep. They would either be spent longing desperately for the next fix or spent in excruciating duplicity with iishana, a falseness her powers of intuition would not take long to penetrate.

And then what? She would kick me out. My finances were delicately arranged to cover the living expenses of a shared household. We shared a car, her car. That would be gone. I began to think of my kids. They came across the state every weekend to stay with me. How would I get them? Where would they stay?

Sitting in that terrible meeting, I watched as my entire life collapsed in slow motion, like an abandoned high rise brought down by a skilled demolition team.

It was a long day waiting to tell iishana. And the telling felt even longer. These were not easy words to say. It was no fun watching her wince, seeing the pain and anger in her eyes, as I tore down big chunks of the trust we had created together over five years. And, as I spoke, it became clearer and clearer that celibacy was not working for me. While I treasured our tantric connection, I also craved the deeper orgasmic connection we had before we married. Part of our vows was the pledge to pursue a disciplined course of tantra— all sexual energy brought into the upper chakras, no more coming. But now I wasn't so sure. That's part of what had driven me toward Emily.

Even though I could not have found a worse way of telling her that I needed to resume a more traditional sexual relationship, iishana was incredibly understanding. As we looked together at the ugliness of my behavior, the damage it had caused and was on the brink of causing, I was taken back to the day I told Nancy of my infidelities, the dread of having to see myself as Mr. Hyde. And, of course, this took me back to that day in Kentucky, when my mother forced me to stare at the horror in the mirror.

But this time, I was held. Iishana's deep brown eyes stared into mine. She did not look away. Her love continued to wrap around me, like Amma's endless embrace two months before, the way She stayed with Dattan when everyone else wanted to drive him away. I may have been caught in disease-driven behavior, but iishana still loved me. She knew of my struggles with depression and addiction, knew that my demons were part of the package. And she knew I was willing to take the necessary steps.

A few days later, I met with my sponsor. He told me that a different twelve-step program was needed. Ever since my life with Nancy exploded twenty years before, I knew there was some kind of sex addiction afoot, but removing the alcohol seemed to bring it under control. There was no reason to go into a twelve-step program for perverts. I mean, the one I was in was bad enough. Everyone knew it was for losers. Drunks and junkies for God's sake! But one for sex?

In the middle of all this, the Harvey Weinstein story broke. And, to make it even more bizarre, I learned that his first wife had been my first "girlfriend." Nothing serious, I had been thirteen and she was eleven, but we had gone to a dance together at West Chop, on the Vineyard, shared a few special moments. A lot was being said about him seeking treatment for an addiction. I read all the editorials. They were ten to one that this was nonsense. He wasn't sick. He was a complete asshole.

And of course, that is one of the definitions of the disease: "Instant asshole. Just add… " Having any kind of addiction is no excuse. If you have it, you have to deal with it. And while I certainly hadn't raped anybody, I recognized his disease.

When he told one of his coworkers back in the eighties, "I just did something terrible. I don't know what got into me. It won't happen again," he had just given the secret password to our club. And if you haven't suffered from an addiction, you probably won't understand. That's one reason twelve-step programs are so successful. Addicts are pretty much the only folks who understand other addicts. There is a reason we call non-addicts "earthlings." "Muggles" would work just as well.

I have always been what they call in the rooms a "high bottom." The moral and spiritual "bottom," or moment of truth that drove me to into a twelve-step program, was nowhere as bad as it could have been. I never killed anybody, never put my wife or kids in the hospital, but I knew plenty of people who had. That was why I went into recovery in the first place. I could see "jails, institutions and death" in my future. As they say in all the addiction programs, "It's a progressive disease."

I can hear some people say, "Lots of people have affairs, but that doesn't make them sex addicts." And that may be true, if you are not an addict. But, for an addict, the diagnosis is exponential: "One is too many and thousand will never be enough."

What it comes down to, as a wise friend of mine often says, is that alcoholics and addicts are terrified of pain. They would rather do almost anything to avoid sitting with their emotions, especially the ones that hurt. And that was the first thing I ran into in my new program. There was no miracle cure. No one was going to wave his hands, mutter a few magic words, and take my suffering away. I was going to have to sit with my pain. But at least I could do it in the company of folks who had been there, knew exactly what I was going through.

They call this first period "Withdrawal" and that's exactly what it felt like. Because it wasn't just that I could no longer hang out with Emily. I had to stop thinking about her. Ever. And that was the hardest part. Not being able to think about her, not to be allowed to run that mental tape. Because thinking is at the root of any addiction. An individual thought can seem so harmless, but just like scratching poison ivy, each attempt to soothe the pain only aggravates it.

As I sat with that longing—sometimes a burning in my chest, sometimes a cold feeling under my skull—I was with a familiar companion. In fact, it had been with me as long as I could remember. When I was little, four or five, these feelings would come over me as I tried to go to sleep. Alone in an empty room, I would comfort myself with memories and stories about little girls in my nursery school or kindergarten. Not erotic stories, but romantic stories, of pretty little girls in party dresses, shared moments, maybe, every once in a while, a peck on the cheek.

And these stories had continued. All through grade school when my buddies spoke of how awful girls were, I would nod in agreement, but, every night, I was telling myself those stories. And, as adolescence blossomed, these stories became sexual, fantasies to masturbate to. Even after I became an adult, the emptiness followed me, and the stories came, too. They functioned as a kind of analgesic for the ancient loneliness, masking the symptoms but never coming anywhere near curing the disease.

And this is the essence of being an addict. It really doesn't matter what you are addicted to. In the moment, that substance or activity promises so much, is so convincing, is "cunning, baffling and powerful." Yet, whatever the addiction, the end result is always the same: ruin and desolation. I remember hearing once that the feeling compulsive gamblers seek is not the rush they get when they win, but that horrible empty feeling of losing. The payoff isn't pleasure. It's pain.

And this completely resonated with me. I would have told you that I pursued any of my addictive behaviors—alcohol, marijuana, romantic intrigue and sex, food—in order to feel "better." But, if I looked back over my life, going all the way back to the basement hallway, the end result had never been to feel better. Just like my suicidal fantasy on the family cruise, all my addictive behaviors led back to my earliest traumas;

they all reproduced with uncanny accuracy the very feelings I was trying to escape: overwhelming shame and humiliation, loneliness and grief.

The old addict's riff on Einstein—"Insanity is doing the same thing over and over again expecting different results."—began to rework itself in my mind. What if the disease of addiction wasn't insanity at all? What if its ability to recreate, over and over again, the exact same awful results served a purpose? Like a dog who keeps pulling his owner in a certain direction, like the dog that kept scratching on the bathroom door behind which a friend of mine had overdosed, was silently dying, until the dog's owner became annoyed enough to open that door, see his friend going into a coma, call 911.

What if the dis-ease of addictive longing is an expression of a similar undying loyalty and faithfulness, determined to bring our awareness back to certain moments in our life we have done everything in our power to forget? I thought of my experience at the Tibetan Buddhist retreat center in Ireland—when I felt deeply into my agony at being abruptly weaned – it connected me to Jamyang Khyentse, who had been suffering in a much larger way during that same week in 1959, right before he died. And how that connection set me free for a little while.

Those feelings of joy and liberation took me back to my first vision quest when I had my first experience of *ananda*, the limitless joy of being. And how had I arrived at that state? By intentionally entering a state of complete abandonment—not just alone in the wilderness, but without food or water for several days. Could an adult more closely replicate an infant's experience of being abruptly weaned, of being left alone for hours and hours and hours?

It wasn't the abandonment that took me into bliss. It was the moment of complete silence I finally arrived at after my mind had run through all its thoughts about what abandonment meant.

There is precedent for this apparent irony. Many spiritual traditions talk about the need for complete surrender in order to fully experience God's love. In the Gospel of Thomas, Jesus says we must become as "suckling infants" if we want to enter the Kingdom of Heaven. In the Lakota *hanbleicya* (literally, "crying for a vision"), participants will climb the sacred mountain on their knees, actually weeping, saying over and over again that they are hungry, powerless, desperate. Rumi, in his poem, Love Dogs, advises his readers to become like that neighbor's dog, howling for his absent master. "That cry is the connection."

And this is what Amma's lead swami would recommend every year in his talks. He always described how he began every day, "like a little child, crying out "Ma, Ma, Ma!" And I remembered thinking every time, "That's ridiculous. I'm a grown man. No way am I going to pray like that."

But, grown man or not, I found myself in the rooms of another twelve-step program, pressed up against my behaviors of the last half century, which, again and again and again, had brought me to the brink of suicide, wrecked my marriages, and showed no sign of ever abating. In recovery, they call this "the gift of desperation," the bottom, the place where you are brought to your knees. Denial is useless. There is nowhere to run. You have come to the end of the road.

My mother suffered terribly from post-traumatic stress disorder and her abuse left me with a similar trauma. However, PTSD never showed up as violence in me. I never hit or threatened anyone. I had no problem with diapers with my kids— shared duties 50/50 with their moms, never felt a need to "toilet train" them— such an awful term— just gentleness and patience. Poop wasn't a trigger for me like it was for my mother.

My PTSD showed up as "repetition compulsion"— repeatedly engaging in behavior that was guaranteed to lead me to being held in front of a mirror, "shit" all over my face— my current partner outraged, my community gossiping about me— outcast again. That was the root of my sex and love addiction. That was where it always led. That was the payoff.

This is why the story of Amma and Dattan the leper moves me so much. We don't have leprosy in the West. We have toxic shame, those feelings of self-loathing that make us feel "like lepers." After Amma's long hug, within days I went into therapy for my sex addiction; within weeks I found the courage to tell iishana; within months I joined a twelve-step program for sex addicts, went to meetings every week, got a sponsor.

A true guru knows everything about you, everything you are thinking. Just like Jesus with the woman at the well. Just like Maharaj-ji with Ram Dass. I knew, as Amma held me that night, that she knew exactly what I was struggling with, how deeply it had its hooks in me. That's why she held me for so long. And the proof of her power lies in what happened after— changes I had been unable to make for fifty years. And Amma would say, just as Jesus did to those he healed, "It was your faith that healed you."

So that became my prayer. Whenever thoughts of Emily arose in my mind, I silently called out "Ma, Ma, Ma!" Instead of telling myself pretty stories, I cried out like a desperate baby. I imagined myself on the changing table, in the crib, in front of that mirror, alone and afraid, and just screamed for my mother. Except now, that mother wasn't the depressed twenty-something who had been overwhelmed by my needs. I was crying out for Amma, Mata Amritānandamayī, the Mother of Immortal Bliss.

Chapter 16

Impregnate Me with Thy Light

It's funny. We think of Winter Solstice, Christmas, New Year's Day and Epiphany as different holidays, but they all celebrate the same thing: the return of the Light. Whether we gather to give thanks for the Sun returning or the Son arriving, the feeling inside is the same. Whether we celebrate the beginning of a new year or a new era, we feel exhilaration, hope, new possibility. What all these holidays, Holy Days, share is an awareness that a period of darkness is ending and a new period of light is beginning.

As I began my sexual sobriety, I felt tremendous relief. Something terrifying had been stalking me for decades and I had finally turned to face it. The endless "looping" could finally end. All I needed to do was embrace the longing instead of running away. All I needed to do was surrender, cry out "Ma, Ma, Ma!" over and over and over. It wasn't always easy. Who wants to return to such helplessness, such aloneness, again and again? Except now I could now see the alternative very clearly. The price of running. Tibetan Buddhist master, Pema Chodron, calls this clarity "the wisdom of no escape."

That December, my mother fell and broke her hip. Because I lived nearest to her, I was the first to go to her bedside in the hospital. By odd coincidence, iishana and I had already planned to stay at her house that same night: it was the eve of the Winter Solstice and we had made special plans.

Near where my mother lives is Calendar II, one of the biggest and best-known stone chambers in New England, measuring ten feet by twenty feet. This ratio of 2:1 is found in the King's chamber of the Great Pyramid. Its ceiling is formed from seven massive lintel stones, the largest weighing three tons. No one knows who built it or why anyone would carry such huge stones to the top of a hill. But one fact is known: the door to the chamber is oriented so that the rising sun shines directly inside on the Winter Solstice.

Two months earlier, iishana and I planned with a couple of friends to make a pilgrimage to Calendar II on this most holy morning. So I was struck to get my mother's call the day before the winter solstice with her unfortunate news. My mother and I had visited this site a couple of times before during warmer times of year. She believed it was a Goddess Temple, a relic of an earlier matriarchal period.

In fact, she had been schooling me about the Matriarchy since I was a teenager, gifting me with the Jungian classic, *The Great Mother* by Erich Neumann, when I was seventeen, a book which I devoured and which had a huge impact on my understanding of history. That was the same year my shaman uncle informed me that I had been "initiated in the mysteries of the goddess." He was referring to my relationship with my mother—both the early trauma and our deep connection— but I had no idea what he was talking about. However, over the years, Ellis's words came back to me again and again.

Even though I suffered terribly at my mother's hands (as she had suffered with her own parents), we had always been very close. Where my dad represented authority and status and reliability, my mother was a rebel. My dad always felt distant, but I could talk about almost anything

213

with my mom.   And while I was not entirely ready to accept everything she said about the Matriarchy, I knew for damn sure the Patriarchy was never going to work for me.

Another difference between my parents was their willingness to reflect and change.   When I confronted my dad about his failings as a parent, the farthest he could go in acknowledging them was to say, "I guess if I wasn't part of the solution, I was part of the problem." Forget admitting to any cruelty or negligence.   But ever since my parents' divorce in 1970, my mother had continuously delved into her abuse, both her suffering at the hands of her parents and the pain she had caused.   My dad rarely spoke of such matters, never to my knowledge sought professional help, but my mother put in long hours of therapy and alternative modalities and was always willing to process the past with my siblings and me.   She never shied away from taking responsibility and was heartfelt in her apologies.   I always felt heard and seen and validated by my mother and she has been an enormous inspiration in my own healing journey.   Her ability to courageously transform herself over the decades showed a way forward for me and gave me great hope.

So when she broke her hip, I was concerned and also grateful that iishana and I could stay at her home to be near her.   And, following my mother's earlier inspiration regarding myth and ancient wisdom, iishana and I arose in the freezing dark on Solstice morning and made our way to the top of a hill in South Woodstock, Vermont. There was already a small group gathered around the chamber's entrance when we arrived. It was a little below zero and everyone stomped their feet and hugged themselves to stay warm in front of the small black opening to the chamber.

It looked just like one of the megalithic ceremonial chambers I had always been drawn to in England and Ireland. The doorway was a black hole which also reminded me of the door to a sweat lodge, an opening to the unconscious or the Lower World. Around the opening, the earth swelled like an enormous loaf of bread, its top covered with snow, large rocks peeking out from the sides. One by one, we went into the darkness.

There were a dozen of us, each drawn by some kind of mystery. I spotted a couple of folks I knew outside, but inside we were all strangers and family. I couldn't see anyone's face in the gloom, but only kin would be crazy enough to be sitting here in the predawn cold and darkness. As we sat together in the freezing silence, a gray light began to appear outside the entrance. Trees took shape and color began to glimmer in the sky beyond, pinks and oranges.

When the moment came, there was a collective gasp. An enormous pot of molten honey was slowly lifted from below the horizon and tipped, poured in a stream toward the chamber entrance. This brilliant, golden light came in a flood across the snow, straight between the great stones at the entrance, straight down the center of the chamber, until it hit the stone wall at the western end. As it first turned the entrance stones into glowing gold, everyone pulled back against the side walls as if they feared they would be burned. As the liquid light ran across the floor, we pulled our feet even further back. It looked like it could set you on fire.

One person summoned up the courage to crane forward to catch a glimpse of the rising sun and her darkened features were suddenly caught in a brilliance that was hard to look at. This light was nothing like the light I was familiar with. The contrast between fathomless, icy darkness and sudden illumination gave the light a palpable quality, as if you could catch it with a spoon, plunge your hands into it.

Words formed in my mind, a prayer:

Impregnate me with thy light, that I might shine unto the people and bid them do likewise.

I had no idea what these words meant, but I repeated them in my mind as I watched my companions take turns leaning their heads forward to behold the sun and be transformed. It was as if I had never really known what light actually was until this moment, never known what it could do.

Over the next few months, my sister, Anne, and I took turns staying with my mother, helping her arrange for nursing care, go to doctor's appointments. The "pin" they put in her leg, I saw in the x ray, was actually a four-inch lag bolt, like something you would use to hold a deck together. My mother's very structure had been altered and my sister and I were changed into stewards of her new vulnerability.

We talked about this, reminisced about how she had had sometimes treated us when we were helpless in her care. Now the shoe was on the other foot. How would it be?

It was a very special, tender time for all of us. Anne and I took turns spending weekends with my mother, who had a home health care aid with her during the week. My mom was so vulnerable, so grateful for our kindness. We all knew a seismic shift was occurring and we were patient with one another as we learned the new steps.

Things had just stabilized with my mother—the cast was off and she was starting to walk again—when the phone rang. It was one of the leaders of the New England Amma Satsang. Swami Ramanand-ji would be coming to Brattleboro the following Friday. We needed to book a church. As it turned out, that particular Friday fell during Easter week and no local churches had any space available. We would have to host the swami in our yurt.

Amma had a number of swamis, ochre clad, celibate bramacharis; she called them her "wives." To have one of these men come to our yurt would be like having one of the Pope's top cardinals come to your church if you were a Catholic. No one ever explained to us exactly why he was coming, but members of the New England satsang assured us this was a great honor, not one conferred upon all satsangs, and that we were receiving a great blessing.

And, certainly, when Bramachari Ramanand-ji, clad all in white that day, poured into our yurt with his entourage of young Americans and older Indian ladies, we felt something. As he sat beside the large picture of Amma, who was also dressed in white, also had glowing brown skin, it was if our guru's son was with us. Before beginning the bhajans, sacred songs, Ramanand-ji spoke of how Amma first came to America and then to Boston. "And now," he said, looking directly at iishana and me, "She is here in Brattleboro." Even though Amma herself was at that moment in her ashram in India, we both felt her enter the yurt to be with us.

Iishana and I had been feeling that it was time to move out of the yurt and turn it into a dedicated temple space and after Ramanand-ji left, we got to it. A renter had recently moved out of iishana's house so a room was available for us. Part of me did not want to leave the yurt. Living in a house with running water and plumbing again after so many years felt like selling out, succumbing to civilization, but iishana was ready to return to having basic amenities. And now, Amma had come to us herself! We needed to step up.

At this time, spring of 2018, iishana and I were becoming more and more concerned about the opiate epidemic that was devastating our little town. Over the past six weeks, four people we knew personally or who were friends or relatives of friends of ours had died from overdoses. We were middle-aged teetotalers. It wasn't like we hung out with drug users. In a town of eight thousand, this was a terrifying mortality rate.

As I listened to the news, to gossip, it felt like we were only talking about the tip of something much larger, an epidemic of despair. This awareness, that we were beset by epidemic loss of hope about the future, became the focus of my prayer. What could I do in my small way to help alleviate this epidemic?

A way to answer this question arrived in mid-June of 2018. I was part of a local men's group, eight men in their forties and fifties who got together every two weeks to talk about their lives, share wisdom and challenges. Elliot, the group's founder, offered his land in Guilford for a two-day men's retreat. He and his wife, Elise, lived on a secluded mountainside where they served as stewards of the land. Sweat lodges were held there frequently and shamans from South America had held many ceremonies there over the years.

Elliot and Elise were one of our favorite couples to hang out with. We were all devotees of Amma and often got together for satsang or to share visions of the world we wanted to create together. Elliot and Elise lived off grid on the site of one of the original Brattleboro communes, alternative communities which sprang up in the sixties, and kept the vibe going by growing all their own food and hosting frequent gatherings, music jams and spiritual ceremonies.

They were informal community leaders and I wasn't surprised when Elliot approached me about creating a men's group in early 2017. It was just the two of us at first, but Elliot, through his wide network of friends, kept inviting people to join and soon there were eight or nine men—musicians, carpenters, trackers. Only one or two had a nine-to-five job.

We scheduled a meeting on Elliot and Elise's land to discuss details of the summer retreat, but just before that meeting, I was walking outside with Elise and two other women, Nancy and Cara, looking for a spot to hold our upcoming Summer Solstice ceremony. It was raining as we walked through the woods, arriving at the place where Elliot and Elise were married twenty-five years before. Several summers earlier, a lightning strike had devastated the large red oak tree there, splintering two of its main branches. An Andean shaman had recently been to visit the land and had been intuitively guided to this spot. He pronounced it an energy "vortex" and we could all feel the power, a thickening of the air, hair rising on our arms, as we approached the devastated oak.

"Elliot worried what the damage meant for our marriage." Elise told us. Her husband had taken the lightning strike on their wedding spot as a bad sign. Nancy wasn't so sure.

"Sometimes power can feel overwhelming," Nancy said. "We can feel overwhelmed, but it's really an invitation to step up." Nancy Crompton was a quiet leader in Brattleboro, a long time Tibetan Buddhist practitioner who helped organize spiritual gatherings from behind the scenes. She never put herself forward, but things seemed to "happen" after she became involved. We took her words in and pondered them in silence.

At that moment, Elliot drove up the long dirt driveway and parked not far from where we standing. He had just come from working in Brattleboro where he had been delayed by a "micro burst," a sudden powerful, tornado-like blast of wind, rain, thunder and lightning. All we had felt out in Guilford was the rain. He was relieved to see we were ok.

As we walked back toward the house, we all agreed the vortex felt too powerful for a gentle community ceremony. Nancy spoke the words I had been thinking, "But what do you do at a place that powerful?"

Later, as Elliot and I and the other men designed the upcoming retreat, we all agreed on an evening sweat lodge followed the next day by a ceremony with sacred mushrooms. I didn't work with hallucinogens much anymore, but, as with the ayhuasca four years before, when I hit a real stumbling block, I knew they could be helpful. My concerns about the "epidemic of despair" felt like such an obstacle. I also had the answer to Nancy's question. I knew where I would be sitting when I took the psilocybin.

When I got home that evening, iishana was in tears. The microburst Elliot told us about had struck close to home. An enormous tree at the back of our property had been ripped down and, in its falling, struck our yurt a terrible blow. Three rafters were shattered, splinters of wood scattered across the floor, the aftermath of an explosion. The impact occurred right above the thangka of Manjushri, the bodhisattva of wisdom. I stood staring at his impassive features. It was as if the flaming sword he brandished above his head had come right through the wall.

One of the shattered rafters hung down into the room, its storm sharpened point ending right at my Adam's apple. It was as if Manjushri had finally lost patience and cut right through the shelter of surface appearances— at the very moment when I had been standing beneath a storm-blasted tree ten miles away trying to divine the message in the damage there. This being was no longer just an image in a painting. He had cut hard into my life.

We had only moved out of the yurt two days earlier. Had we delayed, someone could have been killed. As we surveyed the damage, we noticed that, aside from the three rafters, nothing was broken. A vase of wilting flowers stood, undisturbed, where it had been placed before Manjushri the previous week. Pictures had been knocked off the wall, other objects tipped over, but nothing was damaged. Still, iishana was distraught. Our once cozy home looked like a warzone. I kept hearing Nancy's words from earlier that day. "Power can feel overwhelming, but you are just being invited to step up."

Two weeks later, I took my question to Amma in Marlborough at the convention center she visited each year on her world tour. "What could I do to help heal the epidemic of despair in my community?" I handed her the question, written in English and in her native Malayalam. She looked stricken as she read my words. I could see her feeling the pain I was talking about. Her face filled with compassion, kindness, and her eyes welled with tears. "Keep trying," she said. "Keep trying."

Later that month, Elliot and I ceremonially combined the sacred mushrooms with ground cacao, an ancient Mayan recipe which combined two great contributions of that lost civilization. The eight of us drank the brew in silence, each carrying his question, each on a private quest. We would spend the day alone and then return to the central fire at sunset to share our visions.

I headed to the vortex, to the shattered oak tree. Perhaps in that place of power things would become clear. As I sat at the oak's feet, feeling the mushrooms come over me in waves—shivers, flashes of brilliant color, an energy which threatened to overwhelm—I was struck by clarity. The answer to my question was so obvious there was almost nothing to it. The way to help heal the epidemic of despair was simple— become immune to it! Despair was not in any way real. That loss of hope— despair is from Latin desperare, "to be without hope"— was a child's fear of shadows, a flinching before imaginary monsters. Despair was a phantom.

This was a place I had been before. St. Therese of Lisieux summed it up as "Everything is grace." Joshu Satsai Roshi, Leonard Cohen's teacher at the monastery on Mt. Baldy, expressed this awareness as "The result of everything is true love." I first heard it in the scream of cicadas: "Beeeeeee!" The real challenge lay between our ears, the pervading sense that something was wrong. The only thing wrong was our thinking. As Amma told a friend of mine who suffered from multiple addictions, "You will find the cure for your disease in the spaces between your thoughts."

Mushrooms made it so easy. Instead of a long hard climb to the top of the mountain that took years, lifetimes, you were taken to knowing in moments. I knew what I was being shown—what I was feeling with complete clarity, complete certainty—would not be so easy to hold on to back in ordinary reality, but this was a fresh awareness. I had been given a clear bearing. A new mission.

Become immune to despair.

Just fixing me seemed selfish and limited. How would that help a community in despair? But as I sat with these new instructions, their wisdom sank in. How can I hope to help others if I am sick myself? Someone actively infected with a disease will do far more harm than good. First things first. Before I could hope to help others in the way I prayed to be able to, I was going to need to do some more house cleaning.

Two weeks later, on Guru Purnima, the full moon of the Guru, the one day of the year when the Guru is a thousand times closer to the devotee, I heard back from our insurance company. It turned out the yurt was included under our homeowner's policy and we were going to receive a little over five thousand dollars, a small fortune in Vermont's thin economy. Since I was a carpenter, I had already figured out how to repair all the storm's damage for just the cost of materials, maybe a thousand dollars. This award meant we could get the yurt ready to be a temple—the Heart Temple.

Iishana had been seeing this in visions for several years—a temple space dedicated to the Heart, to the vibration, awareness, consciousness, which sprang from the fully flowered Heart Chakra. It could be found in all spiritual traditions: the sacred heart of Jesus, bodichitta in Buddhism, the connection between guru and disciple in the Hindu tradition, the place lodge took you. This Temple would not be dedicated to any particular tradition, but instead would celebrate the awakened Heart wherever it occurred.

In her vision, iishana saw altars to all the heart traditions of the world, each set low along the circular walls so you could sit and meditate before it. We knew we wanted to reconfigure the yurt in this way after we moved out the previous month, but had lacked the financial means to do so. The coincident occurrence of Guru Purnima and the insurance company's good news was striking. We saw this synchronicity as a continuation of the sequence begun by the swami's surprise visit three months before, closely followed by the tree striking the yurt. These four separate events felt somehow connected, each a manifestation of Amma's grace. As upsetting as the shattered rafters had been, that blast threw aside the door opened by Ramanand-ji, a door we could now step through.

We redid the floors, had the carpet professionally cleaned, purchased twenty backjack chairs, and were able to afford a large and beautiful carved wooden Buddha from Bali, painted gold in a radiant, joyful expression of the fully awakened heart. On Ganesha Chaturthi, Ganesha's birthday and our wedding anniversary, we performed a formal temple consecration, called a kumbhabhishekam: the "sprinkling" (abhishekam) of the temple with sacred waters carried in a "water-pot" (kumbha). Using a branch from the Northern White Cedar, Arbor Vitae, Latin for "tree of Life," and water blessed by Amma, we slowly circumambulated the yurt and, before each altar—to the Earth, to Amma and Maharaj-ji, White Buffalo Calf Woman, Buddha, Jesus, Kali— sprinkled water and recited the mantra or prayer of its particular tradition.

The Brattleboro Amma Satsang now had its official new home. It was also a venue for kirtan. Ultimately, we wanted it to be a community resource for people with "ears to hear, eyes to see," people guided to celebrate the wisdom and energy of the heart in whatever form they liked.

In early November, my dear friend, Joshua, came to visit. We had known each other when I was at Spirit Hollow and had quickly become beloved dharma brothers. Strangely enough, our fathers had actually been married to the same woman (#3 for my dad). So, in a way, we actually were brothers.

I met him at the Hartford airport where he was with his wife, Vanessa, and their seven-year old daughter, Paloma, who were waiting to catch a connecting flight home to Oregon. Joshua would stay east a few days longer before rejoining his wife and daughter. Vanessa was spiritual family as well, one of the few people I knew with courage to say that enlightenment was attainable in this lifetime and that this was her goal. So many spiritual seekers don't say this out loud for fear of appearing grasping or arrogant. But one of the fundamental elements of prayer is to ask for what you want. If you sit in a restaurant, but never order, what is going to happen?   Or, to rephrase Vince Lombardi, "Enlightenment isn't the most important thing. It's the only thing."

So even though I only had a few minutes with Vanessa and her daughter, hadn't seen them in over five years, I cut straight to the chase. "How is the enlightenment thing going?" She was delighted. For the next few minutes, the four of us were held in an exquisite golden bubble. The crowds disappeared. The announcer's voice could not be heard. And Vanessa gave me a fast download of her blossoming relationship with Mooji, a beautiful enlightened being from Jamaica, a disciple of Papaji, himself a student of Ramana Maharshi—the great Indian saint whose one instruction to students and devotees was to answer the question, "Who are you?"

Our time together was ending and Paloma, remarkably present for a seven-year old, suddenly joined my and Vanessa's hands and instructed her mother to play the "See, see, see!" game. Our fingers interwoven, eyes locked, Vanessa chanted along with her daughter the repeating phrase, "See! See! See!," along with a series of children's rhymes. With the final repetition of this command, Vanessa's gaze became especially urgent. Her eyes, golden and shining, bored into mine and she tightened her grip on my hands. There was something I had to see.

When I got home, I looked Papaji up in Wikipedia. I knew of his student, Mooji, and his teacher, but little of him. I read his recollection of his transformational encounter with Ramana Maharshi:

He looked at me intently. I could feel that my whole body and mind were being washed with waves of purity. They were being purified by his silent gaze. I could feel him looking intently into my Heart. Under that spellbinding gaze I felt every atom of my body being purified. It was as if a new body were being created for me. A process of transformation was going on—the old body was dying, atom by atom, and a new body was being created in its place. Then, suddenly, I understood. I knew that this man who had spoken to me was, in reality, what I already was, what I had always been. There was a sudden impact of recognition as I became aware of the Self.

As I looked away from the screen, I felt the same impact. That wonderful feeling I received when I was with Amma, hearing stories of Maharaj-ji, connecting deeply with my dear friends at the airport—that feeling was what I was. Perhaps not as loud as the "Beeeee!" on my first vision quest, but the same feeling, the same knowing, the same awareness of Self. And it had always been there.

Papaji's account echoed iishana's dream about the "vibration of hydrogen" and how the guru transformed her disciple. In fact, his words of how Ramana Maharshi transformed him could have been taken verbatim from iishana's soliloquy upon awakening that summer morning three years before.

This shift in awareness went even deeper. A few weeks later, I was reading Les Hixon's remarkable account of meetings with Ramakrishna, the great nineteenth century Bengali saint. As the guru once again exhorted his listeners to drop all pretenses and feel what they really were— the divine, universal Self— it hit me in eleven words:

What I most deeply long for is what I already am.

What I have spent a quarter century searching for, a lifetime longing for, is what I already am, have always been. Following your bliss doesn't just open doors, it takes you to the end of the Way. The word for this place, this state of consciousness, in Sanskrit is Satchitananda, which means, literally, Truth-Consciousness-Bliss. All one. All the time. Bliss isn't something we need to follow. It's what we already are.

Chapter 17

Perfect Joy

I knew getting used to this paradigm shift would take some time, just like learning to walk. As adults, we take this ability for granted. Who can remember how many falls it took, how much doubt? As small children, only familiar with crawling, being able to travel on two legs is an uncertain proposition. We have to rise and fall over and over and sometimes it really hurts.

We usually take this evolutionary leap with our parents and, typically, they can provide the greatest test when it comes to this new way of walking "in the heart" as well. As Ram Dass used to say, "Whenever you start thinking you are enlightened, go spend a week with your family."

Although I wouldn't describe my dad as particularly bliss-oriented, he was an early model for me in his love for the mountains, his love for walking in the woods. He made possible that vivid childhood memory of standing at the summit of Mt. Lafayette, looking out over the Pemigewasset Wilderness.

Every year after that summit, we made a trip into the White Mountains, my brother, John, joining us when he was old enough. My dad was different on those hikes—relaxed, in the moment. He shared that joy generously, the mystery of maps, his enthusiasm for the trail. In so doing, he planted the seeds of a lifelong love for nature in both my brother and me and, fifty years later, the forest, the mountains, are a lodestar for both of us, a place of refuge and inspiration.

Even after we reached adulthood, my brother and I took some memorable trips with our dad—driving cross country on a tour of the National Parks, a trip up the coast of northern California, even a journey to the Scilly Islands off the south of England, where daffodils grow year-round for sale on the London market. During World War II, the town fathers wrote to Churchill and asked him what they could do to contribute to the war effort. "Keep growing flowers," he is said to have replied.

On the Scilly Islands, the landscape was the same as the summits of the Whites—ancient, rounded granite, swept treeless by the wind. What would have been mountain tops in New Hampshire were islands, the forested valleys swallowed by the sea.

As my father progressed into his eighties, he began to fail. His memory had bigger gaps, dates and details began to slip his grasp. First, he was diagnosed with Parkinson's, and then his doctors realized he had NPH (Natural Pressure Hydrocephalus), better known as WWW, Weird, Wacky and Wet, so named for its most obvious side effects— difficulty with thinking, walking and bladder control. This condition was not helped by his increased consumption of alcohol.

By the winter of 2019, it was clear he wasn't going to live much longer, at least not in his right mind. His younger brother, an internist, went to visit him and warned my brother and me that if we wanted to see him and still be able to have a conversation, we should do it sooner rather than later.

My brother, John, a gifted writer of fiction and nonfiction, turned his talents to envisioning a final trip for the three of us. He and I were to fly in from Vancouver and Vermont respectively, pick my dad up in LA, where he lived, and drive together to Yosemite. There we would stay in a nineteenth century lodge in the park, hiking by day and dining and sleeping in luxury at night. My dad was obviously excited by the prospect, though both his wife and brother were skeptical. He was falling more and more.

However, as soon as my dad began to breathe the mountain air, those fears were put to rest. Although we only expected to be taking short hikes on level ground, my father surprised us by hiking uphill for over a mile the first day and over two miles the second day. I was reminded of the scene *in The Lord of the Rings* when Gandalf visits Theoderic, the Rohirrim king, long stupefied by an evil wizard's spell. Gandalf breaks the spell and hands the king his weapon, "Your fingers would remember their old strength better — if they grasped your sword." And just as the king's eyes widened and cleared as he sat upright with new strength and vigor, my father came back to life in the mountains of Yosemite.

The highlight of the trip was the dinner we shared in the Ahwahanee Dining Room, a baronial hall with towering 34-foot high ceilings, enormous pine rafters and trusses, and pillars built with granite boulders—the space lit by immense iron chandeliers. Although built in the twenties, it put us in mind of the larger-than-life explorers from before World War One, men whose journals had inspired my father, who then shared them with us—stories of men who went where no one else had been. Although Muir came to mind, we all had been drawn to the British explorers with their flair for the literary and the tragic. We began to share favorite accounts. Although my father had difficulty processing information about events happening in real time, he was right at home in the past.

The explorer who called most strongly to my father was Robert Scott, leader of the doomed expedition to Antarctica in 1911-12, where not only did he and his men arrive at the South Pole to find they had been

228

beaten by a Swedish expedition, but they all froze to death on the return journey. My father had pored over Scott's journals as a young man, going so far as to write a play about the men's final days while he was in medical school.

It was a haunting story that captured the desolation and despair my dad must have felt as a boy when his own father committed suicide, dark feelings which had always stalked him, just beyond view. My brother and I countered with the Shackleton expedition, our favorite, led by a contemporary of Scott, also to the Antarctic, also fraught with disaster, but where everyone survived. I could see a generational divide, differing story lines about what happens if you throw caution to the wind and chase after the extraordinary.

As was so often the case with my dad, even though the Yosemite trip was going better than we could have hoped, there was a wrinkle. His wife's mother, who had lived with them for many years, had died just a few days before the trip. We had thought of rescheduling, but, after consultation with my father's wife, Susan, it appeared it would be ok to go ahead. She was in charge of the funeral, which was to be held in Minnesota, and coordinating all the details and caring for her failing, falling husband would have been too much.

However, as the trip progressed, my dad talking with his wife each evening, it became clearer and clearer that his absence at the funeral was in no way ok. As the parallel events progressed, Susan became increasingly resentful. The last night of our trip, my father awoke in the middle of the night convinced that a great war was about to begin and he was the only one who knew about it. He was not far off.

All the pleasure and satisfaction of our time in Yosemite drained away as we drove south and my father expressed more and more clearly the trouble he was in with his wife. My brother and I tried to provide advice—buy flowers, be contrite—but we had no idea what we were dealing with. By the time we arrived at my dad's house, Susan had gone to bed. My brother had to catch a dawn flight home, so only my dad and I would be there to mend fences in the morning.

I awoke at five a.m., shortly after my brother left, with the following words in my mind:

Each person's predicament is simply God sitting with them with infinite patience, infinite kindness, infinite wisdom and compassion, infinite love.

I saw, in my mind's eye, the classic Samaritans' graphic—a man or woman, head in hands, complete despair—— but here they were not alone. A presence sat with them, suffused with and radiating enlightened comfort.

Unable to sleep, I got up, made a cup of coffee, and went out onto the terrace overlooking the hills south of LA. The sun was just coming up, birds starting to sing, and even though a multi-million-dollar house with a three car garage and a pool is not my personal idea of paradise, it was pretty sweet.

I went inside for another cup and found my father in the kitchen, highly agitated. "You have to leave. You can have a cup of coffee, but you have to go. We can't talk here. Come back to your bedroom." He headed down the hall and soon I could hear him on the phone with Lyft, nervous, hushed tones. Listening to him with the dispatcher was painful, not just because I was being kicked out, but because it reminded me of trying to tie my shoes while on mushrooms. I couldn't figure out the laces at all and found myself muttering, "The technology, the technology."

Because of my dad's NPH, he had difficulty linking simple strings of concepts—like address, time, destination. The dispatcher was being very patient, but, for my dad, this procedure was as complex as something out of Mission Control. I wasn't entirely sure what would show up.

"And I think I have some Frequent Lodger Nights at the LAX Hilton," my dad muttered to me. "I think I can get you in there."

I had been planning to stay with my father for another two days, seeing as it was perhaps the last time we would be together. It was dawning on me that, in fact, I was going to be spending that time at the airport. If I was lucky, it wouldn't be on my dime.

This transaction was even more painful to witness than the Lyft negotiation, a lot more moving parts; however, there was nothing I could do. I drank my coffee and contemplated my predicament. There was no doubt I had behaved outrageously on occasion during the course of my life, but, for whatever reason, no one—not parents, not bartenders, not even wives—had ever thrown me out like this. What was I going to do for two days with no money? I had spent all the money I possessed on flying to California and staking my dad to expensive dinners in Yosemite (my brother covered the lodge). I had been counting on him for the next two days of room and board.

After my father was off the phone, apparently having reserved me a room (at least that was taken care of), I asked him, "What is going on?"

"Susan is very upset. It would be much better if you weren't here when she wakes up."

"Can't we all sit down and talk?"

"No. That wouldn't be possible." His tone was clear.

Out on the street, we waited together in awkward silence. There wasn't much to say. My mind was going a million different directions—outrage, hurt, confusion. What I noticed most though was the expression on my dad's face. He was terrified. Like a small boy who has broken his mother's favorite vase, he was in deep trouble and completely alone with it. It was almost as if I weren't there at all, my existence as his son reduced to a complex technical problem which he had barely been able to solve.

The Lyft car arrived, a boxy gray Ford from the nineties. My father and I said a quick goodbye and I was in the car, swept away as if by a flood. Looking through the rearview window, I saw my dad disappear into the house. For a moment, I was twelve and staring out the back window of my mom's VW station wagon as she drove me and my brothers and sister away from our childhood home in Cambridge for the final time. I was staring at my father walking away from us, up the path to the house, his shoulders hunched. That had been when it really hit me: my parents would never be together again.

And then that image passed and I heard in my mind my father speak the last line of the play he had written as a young man, inspired by the final journal entry of one of the members of the doomed Scott expedition, "I am just going outside and may be some time."

I stare at the back of the driver's head, his hair in a graying ponytail. I dread the next sixty minutes. The last thing I want to do is make small talk.

"You can put on the radio," I suggest. "Any station would be fine."

He doesn't take the hint, looks at me in the rearview. "Are you a musician?"

I wasn't expecting that. "Uh, yeah, I used to play the bass, long time ago though." I pause in the uncertain silence. I can't help myself. "Do you play an instrument?"

He makes eye contact with me again in the mirror. "Yes. I play the Persian drum."

I have never heard of such an instrument, instinctively ask, "Are you from Persia?"

"Yes. I have been here since 1979."

Loss, regret, resignation, pride. Our eyes meet again. I notice how deep and kind his are. I feel a wave of compassion and a deep sense of history—a shared history— tangled, painful, yet somehow filled with hope.

I blurt out something about how sorry I am about how my country had interfered with his. "We should never have gone after Mossadegh in the fifties. It threw your country into a chaos it still hasn't recovered from."

Our gaze meets again in the mirror. Again, I notice his eyes, deep brown, suffused with kindness. "Why do you think people do things like that?" he asks.

I feel a strange sensation in the pit of my stomach, like when an elevator drops quickly.

I am in the middle of the spring semester at the local community college, teaching a class on Native American history. The driver's question triggers an immediate answer, a quote I have been discussing with my students, attributed to Cortez. The Aztec emperor, Montezuma, could not understand why, when the Spanish had the power to demand anything they wanted, they were so fixated on gold. It might be pretty to look at, soft and easily formed into jewelry, but it made no sense that these godmen were so preoccupied with this otherwise worthless metal.

"We have a certayne disease of the harte," Cortez is said to have replied. "And golde healpeth us."

Although I have known of this quote for many years, recently it has revealed itself as the clearest explanation of why things had gone so

233

terribly wrong between Europeans and Native Americans: a disease of the heart and a deeply flawed notion of the cure.

The driver nods thoughtfully. "Yes, that is indeed a terrible disease. One that has caused so much suffering." He pauses. "Do you think there is a cure?"

The feeling in my stomach has expanded into an energy that fills the car. The air feels thick, charged. It holds me in a strangely comforting way. "Ah, yes, I do." I pause before breaching all conventions regarding conversations with strangers.

"Love. Love is the cure. I mean, not romantic love, or even a parent's love for her child. A much larger love, one that includes everyone, everything. That has no conditions."

There is another pause as he regards me in the mirror. "Yes, I agree with you. In my country, we have known about this kind of love for many centuries. You have heard of Rumi?"

I nod. "Of course!"

"He is only the best known. There were four others. Five all together."

I am not sure what he means. "Four others?"

"Yes. Four other poets. The Great Five we call them. Rumi, Hafiz, Saadi, Ferdowsi and Nizami."

"I have heard of Hafiz, but not the others."

The driver smiles. "Get out your pen. Write them down."

He patiently sounds out and spells the names as I scribble on a scrap of paper. "These men were all great doctors for your disease."

By this point, the driver is no longer a stranger. He knows of this larger love, lives within it, and is wrapping me in it as well.

I ask his name.

"Joe," he replies.

"What is your Persian name?"

He smiles. "Javad."

"What does that mean?"

"Generous."

I am no longer in a cab. We have moved into some other vehicle, one of those folktales I loved as a child where the old man you met along the road wasn't just an old man. A mountain maybe, or God.

We laugh at how perfect his name is. Generous. In a few moments, he has more than doubled my awareness of Persian poetry, my access to the true medicine for the heart.

I shyly ask if I could share my favorite line of Rumi. He nods, smiles.

Rain fell on one man.
He ran inside his house.
But the swan spread his wings and said,
"Pour more on me of that power I am fashioned from.

Javad is delighted. "I didn't know that one. Say it again."

I repeat it and then he asks me, "Say it again." And then, "You must write that down for me. It is very good."

As I write the words on the piece of paper he hands me, I reflect on the absurdity of this scene: me, an ignorant American, writing down the translated words of the great poet for a man who can read Rumi in the original. Just the same, Javad seems so pleased, repeating, "It is good. Yes, it is very good!"

Before I know it, we are at the airport. As I get out of the car, Javad comes around to where I am standing, embraces me, kisses me on both cheeks. "We are like brothers."

I nod, my eyes glistening. He is indeed my family, but in a much larger sense of the word.

I enter the Hilton lobby. Back in the world.

In his confusion, my father has booked the room in his own name. The receptionist looks at me suspiciously. "We can't just give you this room. It's not in your name." It occurs to me that if I hadn't changed my name, I wouldn't be in this fix.

Fortunately, my dad picks up on the third ring. He is a little confused to be hearing from me, but he appears to understand what I am telling him. Twenty minutes later, I am in my room, number 7013, with a lovely view of the airport. It is eight a.m.. My flight is for eleven-thirty p.m. the next day. I settle in and pick up the book I'm reading: a biography of St. Francis.

The author is describing a legendary scene from the life of Saint Francis. It is winter and he makes his way through the cold to one of the churches he famously rebuilt, Saint Mary of the Angels, in the plain at the foot of the hill of Assisi. Francis is engaged in a soliloquy about "perfect joy," how even if his friars "should give, in all lands, a great example of holiness and edification," that would not be perfect joy. He continues,

"[I]f the Friars Minor were to make the lame to walk, if they should make straight the crooked, chase away demons, give sight to the blind, hearing to the deaf, speech to the dumb, and, what is even a far greater work, if they should raise the dead after four days, write that this would not be perfect joy."
(from *Little Flowers of St. Francis*)

Francis goes on to say that even if his friars were to convert all the Infidels to Christianity, even that wouldn't be perfect joy.

Finally, his companion, Brother Leo, who has been silent up to this point, interrupts to ask what would be perfect joy? Francis smiles and answers that if, upon reaching their destination, the porter refused them entrance, accused them of being imposters and thieves, and left them outside cold and wet and hungry,

if we accept such injustice, such cruelty and such contempt with patience, without being ruffled and without murmuring, believing with humility and charity that the porter really knows us, and that it is God who maketh him to speak thus against us, write down, O Brother Leo, that this is perfect joy.
(ibid.)

St. Francis' destination in this story, the chapel and convent of St. Mary of the Angels, is called in Spanish, *Nuestra Señora de los Angeles*, which is where the city of Los Angeles gets its name. Rumi and Francis were contemporaries and both travelled to the Holy Land. We know they actually passed within a hundred miles of each other at one point and it is conceivable they could have met. I look at the page number of this passage: 173, the same numbers as my hotel room.

I put the book down. My Uncle Ellis's Ozark saying is in my mind:

If it happens once, coincidence. If it happens twice, happenstance. But if it happens three times? Face it, Jack, somebody's shootin' at you.

The words I had awoken to that morning, a lifetime ago, about how every predicament is simply God lovingly tending us. My father kicking me out. The deep connection with Javad. The Rumi quote. And now Francis' hypothetical about being thrown out of a place where you expected to be welcomed. Perfect joy.

My mind can think of a half dozen reasons to be upset at and for my father. How many times in my life had it felt like he was throwing me out? When he sent me away to Andover after my delinquency became too much to handle. His shaming of me when I was caught smoking in the graduation procession. His comment that a real writer needs to be published by twenty-five at the latest, when I was twenty-six. Again and again, he had made it clear that I did not match up to his expectations, would not be permitted to enter the sheltering warmth of a father's pride. And here I am, kicked out again.

Another part of me, mourns for my father. This is probably my last visit. I had been counting on a couple of days' quiet time with him, a final chance to share again my gratitude for his gifts to me, especially the wonder of the woods and the gift of the twelve steps. Like my mother, my dad had been terribly damaged by his own parents and had hurt me as well. Yet they both managed to share life-sustaining experiences and joys with me, priceless wisdom. Whenever I feel stressed or confused, I go into the woods to get grounded, to seek healing. Twelve-step programs, which my father predisposed me towards with his own admiration for their results, saved my life. I had wanted an opportunity to thank him one more time.

But within this swirl of feelings, a deeper pattern begins to emerge. The awareness I awoke with—that every predicament, no matter how awful, was always evidence of divine compassion—appeared ridiculous on its face. The worst kind of Pollyannah nonsense. Yet the Rumi quote about a swan embracing the storm, inviting its power, in contrast with a man's "normal" response, did much to explain the dream. What might first appear to be overwhelming and destructive circumstances are actually a blessing to be welcomed, an infusion of sacred power. And then St. Francis brought everything together. Even if you are thrown out of a place which, by rights, should take you in, if you can see this painful rejection as divinely ordained, you will experience it as "perfect joy," as grace.

All of these sayings express the irony of "fierce grace," the paradox that what first appears to be senseless cruelty is actually divine intervention. And, taken alone, each of these insights could prove helpful or irritating, or even offensive, depending on your turn of mind. However, occurring in abrupt sequence in a completely unexpected set of ways, these pieces of wisdom enhance and reinforce one another with a dynamic synergy. It isn't 1+1+1, but some kind of exponential acceleration.

God doesn't play favorites. There are not some who are Chosen and others left behind. We are all included in this vast embrace. The only thing is that this Love might sometimes be terrifying or excruciatingly painful. Sometimes it makes no sense. And no one can make you see it or accept it. This awareness comes only through lifetimes of trial and error, endless failures and mistakes. And even then, only through grace. Like when the Lyft driver you have never met before offers you medicine for an incurable disease, embraces you as his brother.

We want our families of origin to be all things— safe harbor, sit-com, a ticker tape parade—but the truth is we have all been wounded, are all, in many ways, blind. How can we ever fully realize these child's dreams? We all, if we care to look deeply within ourselves, if we are willing to be fearless, suffer from some form of Cortez's "disease of the harte." We all have—human beings have—a bottomless longing that has taken us around the world, to the moon, to devour and demand more than the earth herself can provide. What makes this a dis-ease, and sometimes a sickness, is that we ask the impossible of ourselves and others. I can never fill this bottomless longing by myself. Nor can anyone else fill it for me. No amount of "stuff" is going to fill this emptiness. It can only be filled, healed, made whole and holy, if we are able to lift our gazes, open our hearts, to the much larger Love that has created everything, that makes our lives even possible.

Mother Theresa said, "We draw the circle of the family too small." While she was suggesting we expand our love beyond our immediate relatives, her wisdom can be taken another way: a much larger love is available to us when we surrender our hearts to the enormous family that is the entire universe, that is, put simply, "the vibration of hydrogen." This is our true "family of origin," a family that holds us without condition in birth, in death, in all points between and beyond.

I won't learn this until later, but the hotel I am in right now is where Amma stays every year when she comes to Los Angeles on her annual North American tour. Every year, these anonymous rooms are transformed for a few days into an ashram, a sacred sanctuary, and thousands receive embraces from the Mother of Immortal Bliss. And even though I don't know this fact yet, I feel held by an enormous grace, the same all-encompassing love I first remember feeling with my grandmother, Sue, the feeling she spoke of in her in last words, "Why, yes. That would be delightful." This feeling— joy, bliss, limitless love— is what I have been tracking my entire life.

While I might be pissed at my dad for things he has done, grateful for his gifts to me, sad for him in his self-imposed isolation, it is really all the same: grace working its inscrutable, inexorable way on each of us. And in this we are both together and alone. We are both, are all, held by the same infinite grace and, at the same time, completely on our own with how to move within it. As I look out the big picture window at the endlessly dun features of LAX, with many hours left to wait before a plane will take me home, I have good reasons to be upset, angry, worried, disappointed, a thousand complaints   All I feel is joy.

Made in the USA
Monee, IL
12 September 2023

42500676R00152